JEWISH THINKERS

General Editor: Arthur Hertzberg

# Arlosoroff

# Arlosoroff

Shlomo Avineri

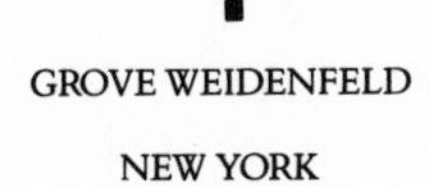

GROVE WEIDENFELD

NEW YORK

Published by Grove Weidenfeld
A division of Wheatland Corporation
841 Broadway
New York, NY 10003-4793

Published in Canada by
General Publishing Company, Ltd.

First published in Great Britain in 1989 by
Peter Halban Publishers Ltd., London

Library of Congress Cataloging-in-Publication Data

Avineri, Shlomo.
Arlosoroff / Shlomo Avineri.—1st ed.
p. cm.—(Jewish thinkers)
Includes bibliographical references.
ISBN 0-8021-1132-7
1. Arlosoroff, Chaim, 1899–1933. 2. Zionism—Philosophy. 3. Nationalism and socialism. I. Title. II. Series.
DS151.A7A95 1989
320.5'4'095694092—dc20
[B] 90-33518
CIP

Manufactured in the United States of America
Printed on acid-free paper
First American Edition 1990
1 3 5 7 9 10 8 6 4 2

For my daughter Maayan

# CONTENTS

# I
# A BRIEF LIFE

On a balmy Friday evening in June 1933, a bespectacled young man of thirty-four went for a stroll with his wife after having a Sabbath meal at a sea-side hotel in Tel Aviv. At an isolated and deserted place along the beach, not far from where the present Hilton Hotel now stands, the couple was accosted by two men. After asking the husband, in Hebrew, for the time and directing a flash-light at his face, one of the two shot him at close range; then both men fled the scene. The wife called for help, but after a few hours the injured man died from his wounds in a Tel Aviv hospital.

The murdered man was Dr Chaim Arlosoroff, one of the leaders of the Labour Zionist Party, Mapai, and at that time Head of the Political Department of the Jewish Agency for Palestine—the Foreign Minister, so to speak, of the Jewish state-in-the-making. Two days earlier, he had returned, via Egypt, from Europe, where he had been planning delicate political negotiations with, among others, the new leaders of the Nazi government in Germany, aimed at allowing German Jews, who were being hounded out of their country, to take with them a fraction of their wealth in German goods when emigrating to Palestine. This initiative, eventually leading to the so-called 'Transfer Agreement' was virulently attacked by the Jewish right wing in Palestine, the Revisionists, who saw it as an ignoble pact with the devil. For Arlosoroff and other moderate Zionists, it was a way to salvage some of the wealth that was being seized from the Jews by the Nazis and to use it for the absorption of the new refugees coming from Germany and for the widening of the economic base of the Jews in Palestine.* For the Revisionist right wing, this undoubtedly controversial policy was seen as treason and betrayal, and its architect—Arlosoroff—was described in some of these attacks on him as a traitor who should be 'eliminated'.

Arlosoroff's murderers were never discovered, though many in Israel have their own personal version of who was responsible. Were they right-wing Revisionists, perhaps on the fringe of Jabotinsky's movement, driven to murder by the incendiary language of some of the attacks on Arlosoroff? Or were they perhaps Arabs from nearby Jaffa, out on a nightly prowl? Was it a political murder, or a botched-up attempt at robbery, or perhaps rape? Nothing is wholly certain, yet *l'Affaire Arlosoroff* was to become the most notorious political murder case in modern Zionist history. It polarized attitudes between left-wing and right-wing Zionists in Eretz Israel and in the Diaspora, led to the final break of Jabotinsky and his followers from the World Zionist Organization, and created an emotional and ideological rift within the nascent Jewish body politic in Palestine, parallel in its intensity perhaps only to the impact of the Dreyfus Affair on French politics.

To the socialist Zionist movement, Arlosoroff became an instant martyr: streets were named after him, a kibbutz (Givat Chaim) established in his memory, as well as a Haifa suburb (Kiryat Chaim). Children were also named after him—and names like Arlosor and Arlosora can still be found, despite their outlandish sound, among Israelis born to Labour parents in the thirties. Arlosoroff was young, brilliant, with a strong appeal as a speaker, and—despite his bookish appearance—quite dashing (a number of romantic escapades were connected with his name, in Germany as well

* The terms Palestine, Eretz Israel and the Land of Israel will be used interchangeably in this volume with reference to the pre-1948 territory of the country.

as in Palestine). In short, he had all the requirements of becoming a hero and a symbol.

As recently as 1982, a noted Israeli writer, Shabtai Teveth (the official biographer of Ben Gurion, and close to the Labour Party), published a book on the Arlosoroff murder case, in which he suggested that one of the Revisionists who was put on trial for the murder but subsequently acquitted, might have, after all, been involved in the assassination. Prime Minister Menachem Begin—the first Revisionist Prime Minister in Israel's history—was so incensed by the allegation that he appointed a Judicial Commission of Enquiry to look into the *Affaire*—fifty years after the event, and when practically all involved had long been dead. As expected, the Commission's Report, which came out in 1985 (after Begin himself had resigned from office in the wake of another Commission of Enquiry), was inconclusive and only added to the mystery. The ghosts of Arlosoroff's assassination had evidently not been wholly exorcized.

In the annals of Zionism, Chaim Arlosoroff is known mainly for the circumstances surrounding his death. For Israeli right-wingers, his name evokes unpleasant memories of an affair in which they have been accused, albeit without conclusive evidence, of political fratricide. For many Israelis of the left, his assassination stands for one of the ugliest moments in the history of Zionism, in which it appeared that one faction of the Zionist movement was moving dangerously into an orbit too reminiscent of what was then happening in Europe. That the year was 1933 only heightened sensitivities on all sides.

Under such conditions, Chaim Arlosoroff the man and the thinker tended to be forgotten. Occasionally the opinion is expressed that had he not been killed at the early age of thirty-four, he might have emerged, after World War II, as the premier leader of the *Yishuv*—the Jewish community in Eretz Israel—and eventually as the first Prime Minister of the

Jewish state. Such speculation, while intriguing, is sometimes off-set by the observation that Arlosoroff was perhaps too much of an intellectual really to make it—in the rough and tumble of Jewish politics in Eretz Israel—to what Disraeli once called 'the top of the greasy pole'.

What is not idle speculation, however, is the fact that besides being one of Mapai's foremost leaders and a Zionist statesman of promise and stature, Arlosoroff was one of the few people in the leadership of the *Yishuv* at that time who was also a European intellectual of the first order and an original social thinker, who had to his name a number of books and many articles in several languages in such varied fields as socialist and anarchist thought, economic history, Jewish social studies, financial theory and social analysis.

It is Arlosoroff the thinker and social theorist, the critical student of Marx, Kropotkin and Nietzsche, a product of Russian populism and German romanticism, that this volume tries to retrieve from the political shadows of the circumstances of his death.

The origins and intellectual provenance of Arlosoroff are as unusual and tragic as was his violent end. His biography epitomizes the burden of a whole generation of Eastern and Central European Jewish intellectuals, who were nurtured, in the vortex of World War I, on the heady concoction of Russian revolutionary thought and German *fin de siècle* romantic idealism, rooted in the Judaic tradition yet estranged from any normative structure of religious Judaism, tossed between Russian and German culture, immersed in both yet alienated from each of them. In short, an archetypal product of that restless Jewish intelligentsia which, in the early twentieth century, turned either to revolutionary socialism or to Zionism—or to both. The unusual character of Arlosoroff, his intellectual brilliance and erudition, only made these traits more powerful, the dosage of this mix higher, the war of the ideas more intensive: so were the inner tension, the achievements, the constant toing and froing.

With a little twist of fortune, and had he been a few years older, he might equally well have emerged as a leader of the Soviet revolution, along with people like Trotsky, Kamenev, Zinoviev, Joffe and Radek. Yet his New Jerusalem was to be in Zion, not in the Kremlin, and it is this route which led him to his end on the sand dunes of Tel Aviv.

Chaim Vitaly Viktor Arlosoroff was born in 1899 in Romny, in the Ukraine, to a middle-class family. He was called Chaim after his maternal great-grandfather, whose son was active in the 1863 Polish insurrection and was imprisoned by the Czarist police; since Russian was spoken at his paternal home, Vitaly (the Russian equivalent to Chaim) was the name by which he was known in his family. Later, when the family moved to Germany, it was changed to Viktor.

As with many other Jews of that generation, these three names reflect the three cultural realms in which the young Arlosoroff was raised. His paternal grandfather, Eliezer Arlosoroff, was the local rabbi in Romny and the author of a number of religious and talmudic commentaries; his father, Saul Arlosoroff, was a product of the Russian Jewish Enlightenment: a prosperous wheat and lumber merchant with international contacts, he was a self-taught man, fluent in Russian and German, as was his wife, Chaim's mother. The circumstances of the family were comfortable, and the home atmosphere combined a relaxed Jewish tradition while acquainting the children with Russian culture.

In 1905, when Arlosoroff was six years old, the wave of pogroms which swept the Russian Empire also reached Romny, and after their house was attacked, the family fled to Germany. They first settled in a small town in East Prussia, not far from the Russian border; in 1912 they moved to Königsberg (since 1945 Kaliningrad, now part of the Soviet Union), where Arlosoroff entered the local *Gymnasium*.

While the family's cultural background continued to be Russian-Jewish, the move to Germany meant, of course, an introduction to German culture, and Arlosoroff's education was in that language. At home, he had a Hebrew tutor.

When the war broke out in 1914, the family—still holding Russian passports—was threatened with deportation and expulsion to Russia. Having fled from there almost a decade ago, they had of course no wish to go back, and succeeded in being allowed to remain in Germany, although they moved to Berlin. When the war dragged on, Arlosoroff's father—cut off from his business contacts in Russia—returned there, via Sweden, in a desperate attempt to salvage some of his assets. He was forced to remain in Russia until the end of the war and then, before he was able to return to Germany, he contracted cholera and died, never having seen his family again. The family thus had to go through the war and the ensuing upheavals in Germany without him.

The move from provincial Königsberg to metropolitan Berlin thrust Arlosoroff into the centre of the hectic war-time atmosphere of the capital, with its large Eastern European Jewish émigré population. The absence of his father must also have hastened the intensity of Arlosoroff's intellectual involvement in the spiritual turbulence of his generation. This involvement proceeded along two parallel lines: the intense immersion in German culture and letters, fostered through the German *Gymnasium* he attended, with its heavy philosophical and literary curriculum; and his involvement in a number of Zionist circles, further study of Hebrew and eventual entry into the Hapoel Hatzair ('Young Worker') socialist Zionist party.

There is a twist, characteristic to the war-time turbulence which moved Arlosoroff towards Zionism. Family members recall that when the war broke out, the fifteen-year-old Arlosoroff, whose German was fluent though still showing the traces of a Russian accent, wanted to volunteer for the German army: so deep was his involvement with German culture that the fact that he and his family were technically Russian subjects did not deter him from feeling totally one with the German nation. Being grateful also to Germany for giving his family asylum in 1905, he had no doubts about his German identity.

Of course he could not join the German army, and the heightened consciousness of the tragedy of the war gradually gave way to an attachment to socialist and universal ideas of human brotherhood—and an equally heightened consciousness of the dilemmas of Jewish identity under the conditions of an international conflict of such enormous dimensions. His teenage turmoil expressed itself in a number of German poems he wrote on Jewish national themes ('Bar Kochba', 'the Maccabees'). Yet the identity problem faced by a young Jewish intellectual of his background is perhaps most hauntingly evoked in a poem called 'To the Jewish War Dead':

> Germany's flag you have loftily hoisted,
> For Russia you rushed into war;
> With French armies you set out to the battle—
> But whose is this war,
> And for whom have you been killed and destroyed?[1]

A similar sentiment is expressed in a letter written in 1917, on graduation, to his German literature teacher at the Berlin *Gymnasium*. He thanked his teacher, with whom he obviously had a close relationship, for all he had learned from him—and particularly for instilling in him, through the writings of Goethe, Kant, Schiller and Kleist, the feeling of duty towards the community. He then added:

> I am a Jew, and I feel strong and proud of my Jewishness. I feel it in my bones that I am different from a German, and it would never occur to me to deny this. I feel how much the Orient is ingrained in me, how much in my soul is a product of an inner rift due to rootlessness ... and unknown to the racial German. On the other hand, I recognize in myself many other

> things which the German thinks are his sole property ... My soul yearns for the unique, ancient Hebrew culture—but I also like German culture, and perhaps I am also afraid to admit how great my love for it is ...
>
> Moreover, sometimes it appears to me that we, the young Jews, who understand what national culture is and who is meant to be the bearer of such a culture, realize more than many Germans how deep are the treasures found in German culture ...
>
> Yet Goethe and Schiller never really touched my heart closely. They fill me with awe and wonder, I get excited by them as by a powerful and magnificent natural phenomenon, which reveals itself to men in all its sublime glory. But I cannot live in them and for them.[2]

Nothing can better express the inner *Zerrissenheit* of the young Arlosoroff as this letter in which his deep attraction to the German cultural heritage is at war with his equally deep feeling of alienation from it. It was as a highly cultured young European intellectual, versed in its rich heritage yet simultaneously looking for his own cultural roots beyond it, that Arlosoroff arrived—like many others in his milieu—at his Zionist convictions.

These convictions were nurtured by a number of sources, among them his acquaintance with Martin Buber, who was then active in Jewish circles in Berlin. Through Buber, Arlosoroff also became acquainted with the writings of Aharon David Gordon, the spiritual mentor of Hapoel Hatzair in Palestine, whose ideas on a 'Religion of Labour' drew on Tolstoyan sources. It was equally through Buber that Arlosoroff got to know the socialist thinker Gustav Landauer, whose anarchistic brand of socialism, inspired by Kropotkin, became one of the more influential sources of social vision in war-torn Germany. In *A Call to Socialism*, Landauer developed a vision of a humanistic, communitarian anarchism, based on a return to nature and agriculture as the only alternative to the violence of modern, industrial and bureaucratized life. It was at that time that Landauer drew near to Zionism, and his vision of a libertarian agrarian socialism became a major inspiration to the kibbutz movement. He was murdered in 1919 by right-wing German nationalists, after having been a member of the short-lived Soviet revolutionary government in Bavaria.

After graduating from his *Gymnasium*, Arlosoroff went on to study economics at Berlin University. By that time he was one of the main leaders of Hapoel Hatzair in Germany and editor of its journal, *Die Arbeit*. It was in this journal that his first articles appeared, next to essays by Buber, Gordon and Landauer—as well as excerpts from the writings of Karl Marx, Pyotr Lavrov, Pierre-Joseph Proudhon and Pyotr Kropotkin.

In 1919 Arlosoroff published his first major treatise, *Jewish People's Socialism* (*Der jüdische Volkssozialismus*). He visited Palestine in 1921, witnessing one of the first anti-Jewish Arab riots there: this immediately drew his attention to the question of Jewish-Arab relations. After his return to Europe, he was instrumental in moving the Third World Conference of Hapoel Hatzair to adopt an explicit socialist programme. In 1923 he presented his doctoral thesis on Marx's concept of class war, and was offered by his teacher, Werner Sombart, a university assistantship. He turned it down, and emigrated to Palestine in 1924.

His political rise in the Zionist movement was rapid. In the 1923 Zionist Congress he was elected to the Zionist Actions Committee, mainly on his record as the author of an influential memorandum on the finances of the Jewish Agency. In 1926 he was sent from Palestine as a member of a three-man delegation to the League of Nations in Geneva (the two other members were Meir Dizengoff, the Mayor of Tel Aviv, and B. Z. Uziel, the Sephardi Chief Rabbi of Tel Aviv, both of them many years his senior). He later visited the United

States for the first time on a fund-raising campaign. Back in Palestine he was instrumental in bringing about, in 1930, the unification of the two main socialist Zionist parties (the Marxist-Borochovite Poalei Zion, and the 'ethical' Gordonite Hapoel Hatzair). With the establishment of this new united party, known as the Mapai Labour Party, he became editor of its intellectual journal, *Achdut Ha'avoda*. At the 1931 Zionist Congress he was elected on the Mapai ticket to the Zionist Executive and appointed Head of the Political Department of the Jewish Agency for Palestine, a position he held with distinction—but not without controversy—until his assassination in 1933.

With his broad European, middle-class culture and university education, Arlosoroff was to become a rather unique phenomenon within the socialist Zionist milieu in Palestine, which was made up mainly of Eastern European pioneering immigrants from the Pale of Settlement, with the *heder* and *shtetl* as their background, rather than a university and a doctorate as in Arlosoroff's case. Most of them had very little knowledge of languages other than Yiddish and Hebrew, and were even less at home in Western European culture. Arlosoroff, very much a star—a *Wunderkind* in his movement—was also to remain, to a certain degree, slightly ill-at-ease within it.

Yet it was his intellectual background and academic training which enabled him to carry on—even during his hectic political involvement, with its frequent trips to Europe and the United States—with his theoretical writing. Spanning a wide spectrum of topics, Arlosoroff's writing have made him one of the major thinkers of the modern Jewish national renaissance and its social reconstruction, combining theory and practice in a synthesis rarely found in either theoreticians or practitioners. Probably only in the formative years of the Russian Revolution can one find his counterparts.

# 2
# CLASS AND NATION

## I

In his treatise *Jewish People's Socialism*,[1] published in 1919, Arlosoroff developed the theoretical foundations of his ideas on the relationship between class structure and nationalism. From this general theory he set out to draw up his programme of socialist Zionism. Written when he was not yet twenty years old, Arlosoroff provides in this essay a surprisingly mature and measured analysis of historical contexts and philosophical considerations, in which his understanding of the dilemmas of the Jewish masses in Eastern Europe—the crucible of Zionism—is closely linked with his general understanding of modern social history and socialist thought. At the same time, the treatise is a penetrating critique of the conventional Marxist views of nationalism. It is also an indictment of the failure of the Second Socialist International to prevent a world war, and a *cri de coeur* of a young believer in a humane, socialist redemption which should find a place in the sun for his persecuted people as well. The treatise's combination of cool historical analysis with fiery social idealism evokes echoes of both Marx's *Communist Manifesto* and Chapter 26 of Machiavelli's *The Prince*, in which the Florentine republican issues his call 'to free Italy from the barbarian yoke'. Surely a strange combination, but it does point to the complexities of both Arlosoroff's personality and argument.

The intellectual background to Arlosoroff's treatise can be

better understood if seen in the context of his studies for his doctoral dissertation, which deal directly with a critique of Marx's theory of class. A condensed version of this doctoral thesis was published in 1925 under the title *Towards a History of Class Warfare*.[2] It should be discussed first, as much of its argument—albeit in a less scholarly fashion than in the thesis itself—found its way into Arlosoroff's treatise on Jewish socialism and served as its theoretical premise.

At the outset of his study of class warfare Arlosoroff maintains that the modern theories of class have themselves undergone a process of change and transformation in response to changing social developments: class theory, Arlosoroff maintains, is as much a scientific theory about social life as it is itself an expression of the social relations it claims to analyse. He then shows at some length how the dramatic events of 1848 have shaped the development of new theories of class. Following Marx, Plekhanov and Michels, Arlosoroff argues that the Marxist theory of class owes much of its structure and content to previous, bourgeois thinkers, especially to Guizot—with one significant difference: in the writings of Guizot and his colleagues it was used to legitimize the bourgeoisie's claim to power, while within the Marxist tradition the same theory was being used as a weapon in the hands of a revolutionary proletarian movement.[3]

Following this dynamic approach to the theories of class, Arlosoroff then subjects the classical theory of class as developed by Marx to such an analysis. He points out that contrary to conventional notions (propagated equally by Marxists and anti-Marxists), Marx himself never clearly stated his definition of class theory. The only instance where he approximates such an attempt (towards the end of vol. III of *Das Kapital*), it is never brought to a successful conclusion, and Marx did not even finish writing this chapter, which breaks off almost in mid-sentence.[4]

Secondly, Arlosoroff argues, Marx's own view of class—even if it was never firmly articulated in a final, fixed formula—did undergo significant changes with time, and as a matter of fact one can discern in Marx *two* distinct theories of class: one expressed in *The Poverty of Philosophy*, *The Communist Manifesto* and *Das Kapital*, vol. I, and the other in his later writings, especially in *Das Kapital*, vol. III.

According to Arlosoroff, there are two main differences in these two phases of Marx's theory of class. In the first and early stage of his writing, class formation in capitalist society is described by Marx as having been basically determined by developments preceding the fully fledged flowering of capitalist society itself: class differentiation between the bourgeois and proletarians is seen as rooted in the process of the rise of capitalism, and the further development of capitalism merely deepens and polarizes already existing differences. It is this line of argument which is summed up in the opening sentences of the *Manifesto* in which all history is subsumed under class warfare, in which different relations to the means of production are at the root of a constant dichotomous view of society (patricians/plebeians, *seigneurs*/vassals, etc.).

Against this view—which has been adopted 'by the priests of the Marxist orthodox church'—Arlosoroff juxtaposes what he sees as Marx's more mature and sophisticated theory. As expounded in the last, unfinished chapter of *Das Kapital*, vol. III, this theory distinguishes *three*, and not *two* classes in modern capitalist society (land-owners, capitalists and proletarians); furthermore, the criterion of social stratification is not the relationship to the means of production, but the differential distribution of the social product.[5]

This is a surprising re-evaluation, according to Arlosoroff, as it suggests that towards the end of his life Marx had re-appraised his bipolar, dichotomous theory of class and found it wanting as being too simplistic. Marx also admitted, according to Arlosoroff, that he had underestimated the role of the land-owning class in modern bourgeois society. Far from being crushed between the hammer of the bourgeoisie and the anvil of the proletariat, the land-owning class (and agriculture as a mode of production) features much more prominently in Marx's later writings and also in his studies about conditions in Russia. Arlosoroff further mentions that Marx's later writings present a much more sophisticated understanding of conditions outside England, whereas his early writings, with dichotomous views of almost total polarization, tend to generalize from merely one case—England—and even here Marx's later writings admit that his earlier picture was simplistic.*

According to Arlosoroff it was the fact that the socialist movement had adopted uncritically the early, and less developed, theories of Marx as its orthodoxy that was responsible for the stagnation characterizing Marxist social analysis. Marxist parties and theoreticians had been repeating *ad nauseam* the simplistic slogan that 'All history is the history of class warfare'—yet, when confronted with real problems of social analysis, the Marxist tradition did not possess an adequate tool for historical understanding. Arlosoroff saw the epitome of such barren scholasticism in attempts by such orthodox Marxists as Plekhanov to re-interpret classical Greek history in the light of a simple-minded and basically primitive dichotomous class structure; on the other hand, he praised the attempts of a younger generation of socialist theoreticians, like Lagerdelle, who challenged these orthodoxies. He concluded that the Marxist movement, while becoming increasingly aware of the limits and tensions of its own tradition, was unable to come up with a more critical and adequate theory of class which would take into account the additional sociological and historical knowledge accumulated since Marx's Manichaean statements in the *Manifesto*.

* Arlosoroff also quotes amusingly from Marx's tract on *Revolution and Counter-Revolution in Germany*, where it is stated that prior to 1848 the following classes existed in Germany: nobles, bourgeois, petit-bourgeois, large- and medium-scale peasants, free small peasants, feudal tenants, agrarian workers, industrial workers (p. 49). So much for 'polarization'.

## II

How does all this relate to Arlosoroff's views on socialism and nationalism?

It was his critique of what he considered the Marxists' faulty understanding of the complexities of class which provided Arlosoroff with his sharpest weapon against what he judged to be the momentous failure of the Second International on the eve of World War I: this failure was due basically to the wholly materialistic reductivism of the Marxist tradition, viewing all social life through the prism of class, and it totally misread the concrete consciousness of the European proletariat. However, this failure of Marxist class analysis should not detract from the redemptive vision of socialist thought, inspired as much of it had been by Marx's intellectual achievements. Like many other post-1914 socialists, Arlosoroff feared that the disillusion with the jejune notions of the Second International might lead to a total rejection of the very vision of a socialist society.

Moreover, Arlosoroff argued that if Marx's analysis failed in explicating the structure of European society in general—how could a mechanistic application of it to the complex social, economic, cultural, religious and national conditions of Jews become a key for a solution?

By calling this essay *Der jüdische Volkssozialismus*, Arlosoroff challenged the undifferentiated universality of orthodox socialist Marxism by evoking two of the intellectual traditions on which he had himself been nurtured: the Russian populist, *narodnik* tradition, so powerful within the Russian, and generally Eastern European, socialist movement; and the German romantic anti-industrialist ideas associated with the *Volk*. That this latter tradition would be, in one of its manifestations, contaminated by its association with Nazism, should not detract from our understanding of the authentic social criticism expressed by it and its emancipatory potential as one of the many intellectual modes of protest against alienation in modern, industrialized society. The Sermon on the Mount and the Inquisition both belong to Christianity, but the horrors of the latter should not diminish one's admiration for the former.

It is this alienation of the worker in modern, industrialized society which is at the root of Arlosoroff's analysis of contemporary life:

> In our time, labour has become soul-less; European and American civilization has mechanized the life of mankind. Everything has become technical. The whole of our humanity has become a huge machine, not an organism, but an organization. Big city culture and division of labour are the names of the twin pillars of the modern temple of idolatry.
>
> Large portions of humanity have been brutally torn away from their relationship to nature, locked up in grey tenements, without air or light, made unable to feel anything nobler than hunger, worry and brutal seeking of pleasure because of their pitiless war for survival. Their own labour they have to carry out in stultifying and deadening huge factories, chained to their machines, at which they have to perform for years and decades the same movement dictated by Taylor's service manual. They thus become themselves nothing other than cogs in the machine. Their work is torn into a thousand minute parts and has thus become senseless and meaningless. The worker has no overview of the totality of what is being produced, and he has consequently no relationship any more to the particle produced by him.[6]

In such a world of crass immersion in materialism Marx, according to Arlosoroff, committed his most colossal mistake: as a reflection of material value in bourgeois society, Marx's own critique of capitalism remained itself imprisoned within this same materialism. Marx's materialist system is to Arlosoroff nothing other than an inverted projection and hypostasis of capitalist values, 'an abstraction of capitalist conditions'. With the followers of Marx, socialism itself became nothing more than 'a question of the stomach' [*Magenfrage*], and 'every development of the soul . . . which has tried to transcend economic interests was crushed under these material necessities.'[7]

It is because of this materialist reductivism that the socialist movement, as inspired by Marx's analysis, was unable to address those human dimensions of the proletariat which transcend economic considerations. The failure of contemporary German social-democracy, wrote Arlosoroff with the year 1918-19 in mind, has to do with the absurd spectacle of workers' clubs where, under the pictures of Karl Marx and Wilhelm Liebknecht, nothing more edifying than card-playing took place and workers could articulate only demands for higher wages and other material concessions.

Arlosoroff argued that socialism had to aim at higher goals. The time had come when workers should stand up and declare:

> We, too, are human beings, with a soul and a right for a soul. We, too, feel; we, too, will. And we shall not blindly obey any mechanical whim. Of course, economic considerations are a significant factor of human history . . . But they have never determined the larger deeds of the human race. Every revolution, every transformation of life, every kind of progress of the peoples, is a victory of an idea for which men fought and for which they sacrificed themselves of their own free will . . . We too have a right to this idealism, for we too wish to mould this world—all of life, both national and social, cultural and religious, according to our ideal.[8]

And it was this blindness to the non-material aspects of human life which had led Marx and his followers, according to Arlosoroff, to under-estimate the national dimension of human life and to the statement that 'the proletarians have no fatherland'. This brought Arlosoroff to the crux of his arguments against orthodox Marxism and to the development of his own views on the role of national consciousness in the socialist movement.

## III

The catastrophe of the Great War—as World War I was called by its contemporaries—transcended the loss of millions of lives, the decimation of whole generations, the misery inflicted on tens of millions of civilians and the unprecedented damage it caused to innumerable cities and villages all over Europe. It also destroyed a way of life, a world of relative stability, a vision of hope for an ameliorated pilgrimage of humanity towards harmony, progress, and individual and social happiness. These visions were shared by conservatives and liberals alike, and though cultural and artistic tendencies towards the end of the century prefigured some malaise underlying this progressivist consensus, what Europe experienced during 1914-18 was so different from all that people had been brought up to expect, that it appeared that the world had become truly unbalanced.

World War I was an even greater shock for the socialist movement and for the Second International, which was led by the major social-democratic parties of Germany, Austria, France and Great Britain. Believing more and more in the gradual diffusion of their ideas, and seeing the steady legitimation of socialist parties within the parliamentary system, had not the representatives of the European working class solemnly vowed that worker would not bear arms against worker? Had they not categorically stated that proletarian solidarity had made war inconceivable—because German workers would never, never fight against French workers? And how could the German war machine, for all its might and the machinations of its generals, admirals and junkers, ever function if the German worker, on whose shoulders the war effort ultimately rested, was never to raise his hand against his brother, the French worker—and vice versa?

Yet within a few weeks during the summer of 1914, this illusion of a world of workers' solidarity as the ultimate guarantee of world peace collapsed ignominiously. Shamefacedly, the leaders of the various social-democratic parties nevertheless voted for the war budgets, following in the steps of the bourgeois and military leaders of their countries, and German, French and British workers proved themselves as jingoistic as any other member of their respective societies.

Marx, Arlosoroff argued, was wrong in claiming that the workers had no fatherland—and hence a movement based on such a fiction had turned out to be a dangerous illusion. The workers may be alienated from the high culture of their society, they may be in bitter conflict with the classes that oppress them: but they were still related to their culture, to its history, its language. Any attempt to substitute this real consciousness of belonging—even if only partially, even if in an alienated and truncated form—to a national culture, would backfire, as it was not based on the real consciousness of the workers. Both the events of 1914-18 all over Europe, as well as the events of 1918-19 in Germany, proved to Arlosoroff that the abstract universalism of the Second International did not correspond to the real consciousness of the workers, nor did it correctly read the historical map. In a language evocative of European romanticism but also reminiscent of Judah Halevi's elegiac tone, Arlosoroff wrote:

> The community of national life and destiny moves the hearts of the workers as strongly as it does that of any other member of society. He too loves his mother's tongue, in which the sparse lullabies were sung to him,

> in which the spirit of his parents lived and created. He too loves his homeland, the people of his homeland, their manifold manners and traditions [*Sitten*], their multicoloured artifacts, the sky of his homeland and the fields and towns of his fatherland. He too carries the culture of his nation within himself: his being, his emotional life, is its being, its life.[9]

Arlosoroff suggested that this 'colour-blindness' of the socialist movement towards the national consciousness of the working-class had, in the past, cost it most dearly in terms of working-class support. Since workers in many cases found themselves alienated by the abstract cosmopolitanism of official socialist attitudes towards their national heritage, they looked for it somewhere else, to the detriment of the socialist movement.

This lesson, Arlosoroff maintained, had at least been partially learnt, and socialist movements were more aware than before that workers, too, relate to the culture in which they have been brought up. But—and here he comes to the heart of the argument—this realization had now been applied 'to French, English, German and Russian socialists. But it seems not to apply to the Jews.'[10]

In order to be truly universalist, he argued, the socialist movement must apply these insights into the cultural dimension of human life to the Jews as well, particularly because of the social climate as it had developed after the war, with a new anti-Semitism spreading throughout society, in which

> ... to the revolutionaries, the Jew is the capitalist, against whom pogroms are instigated; to the capitalist, on the other hand, he is the revolutionary, who should not be allowed to see the light of day.[11]

There had, therefore, to be a Jewish socialist solution to the Jewish problem. But up until then there had been no Jewish socialism, 'though there have been socialist Jews—the Trotskys, the Adlers, the Singers, the Diamants. But it was they, who as good "citizens of the world", fought most passionately against their own people . . . There even exist pseudo-Jewish socialist parties; it is they who have tried to apply alien socialist theories and methods to Jewish life. They have done more harm than good.'[12]

The reason for this lack of Jewish socialism was rooted, according to Arlosoroff, in the specific social conditions of Jewish life, where it appeared that socialists of Jewish origin had been singularly alienated from the experience of the Jewish masses: most of these Jewish socialists came from a middle-class background, where assimilation had been strongest. On the other hand, he acknowledged the contribution of the Bund—the Jewish socialist workers' alliance in Russia and Poland—to the emergence of a Jewish socialist consciousness, as it was 'the first to call upon the Jewish masses to rise for a common cause'.[13] Yet for all its achievements, Arlosoroff argued that the Bund was so imbued with the abstract notions of Marxism that it turned its back on the concrete Jewish historical experience and that even its advocacy of Yiddish came about under the pressure of the masses, not from its original leaders. When in its anthem the Bund declared that 'Judaism and the Messiah are dead', it substituted the abstract entity of a universal proletariat for the concrete identity of the Jewish experience. For all its populism, the Bund was still deeply anchored to the assimilationist ethos of the Enlightenment, which looked at the Jewish heritage as something which was parochial, particularistic and alien—and had to be discarded.

Nations with a rich history, Arlosoroff argued, could allow themselves to discard, in a revolutionary upheaval, the immediate institutional historical contexts of their existence: they could revile church and state, high culture and bourgeois refinement—and yet preserve their identity. The Jews, however, were locked and imprisoned into alien social structures; for this reason, many Jewish revolutionaries, having repudiated the vestiges of their own past, likewise felt no identity with the historical heritage of the people into whose culture they had been assimilated. These Jewish revolutionaries were the only revolutionaries who truly 'have no fatherland'—and they sometimes stood out from their non-Jewish colleagues in their abstract and rootless universalism, denying both their Jewish and their German, Polish or Russian cultural heritage.

Because of the conditions of the Diaspora and the absence of a Jewish 'ruling class', Jewish nationalism was also different from all other nationalisms in being the nationalism of the underdog, of the weak and the powerless:

> Our nationalism is the nationalism of the hungry and the starved. We are all property-less, we are all naked; all of us, as a nation, are a proletarian people.
>
> We do not stoop to conquer, as do those European nations who are proud of their sword; we do not have the power to conquer. We need all the power we can muster in order to survive, to keep our identity, our culture, our being and our future.[14]

The preservation and revival of the Jewish identity could, according to Arlosoroff, be achieved only in a Jewish homeland—and it could be done only in a socialist fashion.

## IV

Why was this the only solution?

To Arlosoroff the reason was not ideological but rooted in the condition of the Jewish masses in the Diaspora. A study of these conditions, according to him, suggested that there was no other alternative: neither the Bundist option, nor a Zionist non-socialist option were viable if one studied carefully what the real Jewish, social and national dilemmas were.

The major misconception attributed by Arlosoroff to the Bund was to imagine that the Marxian schema of the development of classes under capitalism, even if true (and we have seen Arlosoroff's reservations), could be applied to Jewish conditions in Eastern Europe. This referred in the main to the Bund's attempt to depict Jewish social conditions as being polarized, within Jewish society, into a class warfare between a bourgeois and a proletarian class.

Such an analysis of Eastern European Jewish society was utterly faulty according to Arlosoroff. The emergence of a bourgeoisie in European societies was an outcome of a complex historical process where pre-capitalist conditions (free cities, corporations and guilds, an independent peasantry, an urban burgher class) gave rise to what eventually could be called a bourgeoisie. These prior conditions also endowed the bourgeoisie with its economic independence, its ethos of liberty and the traditions of a political struggle for its rights. Such conditions were totally lacking among the Jewish communities in the Eastern European Pale of Settlement. Hence we do not witness there the emergence of a Jewish bourgeois class, though there were individual Jewish merchants and there may have been some Jewish commercial and financial capital, but hardly any industrial capital. Even the existing Jewish commercial and financial capital was not concentrated, had no prospects of ever winning state power (the obvious aim of every bourgeois class), and Jewish employers found themselves employing almost exclusively Jewish workers, with Polish industrialists employing practically no Jews.[15]

Likewise, Arlosoroff argued, a Jewish industrial proletariat hardly existed in the *shtetl*—and Bundists and Zionist Marxists of the Borochovite Poalei Zion movement were equally wrong in maintaining that it did. Because Marxism said that society was divided into capitalists and proletarians, the fallacy occurred that one had to look for Jewish capitalists and for Jewish proletarians. But the working class, which in other societies was the largest and hence the strongest class, did not exist as such among Eastern European Jews. What did exist was a class which was neither bourgeois nor proletarian—whose existence is determined as much by its national being as by it social position:

> The wide Jewish masses are made up of people who are at the same time both property owners and workers: it is made up of people who, while possessing some means of production, cannot, however, survive without their own labour, and are dependent also on their own manual work. The wide Jewish masses thus live in this demi-monde of a petty capitalist economic mode.[16]

The real conditions of these petty entrepreneurs and their employees were almost the same, and did not fit into the neat classifications of class conditions in industrialized societies:

> [The Jewish employer] lives the same kind of life as his apprentice. They share the same room, the same work-table. All the worries of the apprentice are also his worries, with one difference: that the worker has at least guaranteed, through his work, his meagre wages, while 'the independent entrepreneur' is not able to make a profit precisely because of these wages and other costs of production.[17]

In the Diaspora there could be no real Jewish bourgeoisie and no real Jewish proletariat—because society was controlled by non-Jews. Jewish employers found their products boycotted by non-Jewish consumers, and Jewish workers found themselves excluded from non-Jewish factories by non-Jewish workers who in this way expressed their own *national* solidarity by petitioning their employers not to hire Jewish workers: no class analysis of such a complex situation made any sense. Under such conditions of utter powerlessness for both Jewish employer and worker, it was in the grey zone between the classes that the Jews existed: the artisan, who worked with a few apprentices, each of whom was hoping that one day he would be the master, and the employer constantly fearing that he might be thrown back into the position of an employed worker, all living in conditions of a national minority. Marxist class analysis was not very helpful in understanding such conditions.

Moreover, a Jewish entrepreneur, be he (as Arlosoroff says) 'in Lodz or in New York', who succeeded in expanding his enterprise, did not by this expansion strengthen the *Jewish* economy, but the Polish (or American) economy—because a Jewish economy did not exist, and a class war cannot take place in the context of an economy that does not exist.

If no real Jewish bourgeoisie existed, nor a real Jewish proletariat, what does class warfare mean in such a context? Who should be fighting whom? In such conditions, socialist emancipation could not, according to Arlosoroff, mean anything other than emancipation from the foreign national domination under which all Jews, 'capitalists' and 'proletarians' alike, live:

> For us, the victory of socialism does not mean primarily a victory of one class over another, socialist struggle does not mean the struggle of one class against another. Our goal is the positive economic construction of society, the creation of that kind of socialist consciousness which social democracy can create in Germany and Russia only after the revolution.[18]

Jewish social conditions, then, called not for a transformation of an existing society and the changing of the roles of the dominating and the dominated—but *for building an altogether new society*. Jewish society did not exist because of foreign domination:

> With the Jewish people, no class possesses the political hegemony possessed for example by the European bourgeoisie before the Russian and German revolutions. Hence no class can aspire—as the European proletariat does—to conquer this power, as it does not exist . . .
>
> Secondly, all political questions of the Jewish present are not questions that can be addressed to a class or answered by a class. The plunderers and murderers of Lemberg and Kishinev did not ask for means of production or class affiliation. The Jew was killed because he was a Jew.[19]

If class analysis could not supply an answer, what would be the social groups that could contribute to the building of such a Jewish, socialist society?

Because of the conditions of Jewish life in the Diaspora, Jewish social groups could not be determined solely by their class positions. In Eastern Europe, a Jewish employer and a Jewish employee were first of all Jews and considered as such within the context of their society, by Jew and Gentile alike. The fluidity of Jewish occupations and class structures in Eastern Europe meant that the components of such a 'constructivist' Jewish socialism would have to be mixed and varied. While in Russian society, the backbone of the Social Revolutionary party and the *narodniks* was the peasant, in the Jewish case it would be 'the toiling masses'—small craftsmen and their apprentices, those who work in the small home industries, journey-men and small shop-keepers. But the transformation would not, and could not, occur in the Diaspora, where Jews had no chance of being in control of either their destiny or their culture. The roots of Jewish socialism were hence not class roots, as in the Jewish Pale of Settlement 'class contradictions do not exist'. The roots of Jewish socialism were popular and national—

> ... and Palestine, the focus of our newly-awakened creative spirit, the homeland to which our restless nation sets itself to return—it will receive all classes, splinters, tendencies and directions of our people. It cannot, it will not, represent or tolerate the interest of merely one part or one class or stratum of the people.[20]

## V

Thus far Arlosoroff's account tried to explain why a class analysis of Jewish life in the Diaspora was inadequate. He next set out to provide the rationale for the linkage of the social and the national aspects in the construction of a new Jewish society in Palestine.

The distorted nature of Jewish social and economic life in the Diaspora went back to the lack of primary production among the Jews, originating in the fact that there could be no Jewish peasantry under the conditions of living in exile: if you have no territory, you cannot own land. This was determined by the national, not the social, conditions of Jewish life, Arlosoroff maintained and continued:

> The day on which the Roman cohorts set the flame of their hatred to the Judaic holy shrines [was also] the day which uprooted those heroes, who survived the massacres, from their native land; it has torn the Jewish peasant from his soil and sent him into exile. Since then the Jewish people has been separated from its land, there has been no Jewish sowing and no Jewish harvest; hence no Jewish homeland.[21]

Because of his socialist background, and the centrality of labour in socialist thought, Arlosoroff is more radical than many other Zionist thinkers in his critique of Jewish unproductivity. The Jews had become a nation of 'middlemen, agents, jobbers and mediators', of *Luftmenschen*, and thus totally alienated from the mainspring of human existence—labour. Following both the Marxian tradition as well as A. D. Gordon's writings about the centrality of labour in human development, Arlosoroff maintained that Jews had become a paradigm of alienated man; if other groups in society have become, through industrialization, alienated from certain forms of labour or certain aspects of it, it was *the Jews as a nation* who were totally alienated from productive work. If in Eastern Europe this meant the kind of vegetative life of the marginal lower classes, in Central and Western Europe this meant the undue concentration of Jews in the professions and 'literary classes'—and, consequently, a massive unemployment of a vast Jewish intelligentsia—'that intellectual proletariat filling the literary coffee-houses of Berlin, Vienna and Prague, those starving Jewish doctors and lawyers' who also threatened, by their sheer numbers, their non-Jewish counterparts and thus caused friction and anti-Semitic tensions.[22] According to Arlosoroff, similar tendencies could also be found among Jewish immigrants in America, where Jews gravitated within one generation from semi-proletarian to middle-class occupations.

It was this social stratification of ghettoized, segregated life which had stifled Jewish productivity in the spiritual sense as well, and this could not be rectified until the economic infra-structure was set straight: all Jews had to be brought back to work, and this could be done only in a society which would be an overall Jewish society—as well as in a society which would be under Jewish control.

Thus the return to Palestine meant also to Arlosoroff a return to work, and this could be achieved only through a structural transformation of the occupational patterns of Jewish society as it would develop in the ancestral land. In a first of many instances, Arlosoroff voiced in his essay on Jewish socialism the categorical demand that the Jewish settlement of Palestine be founded on Jewish labour. He castigated the settlers of the First Aliyah for thinking that the mere *possession* of land would suffice for a national renaissance: labour had also to be done by Jews, not by cheap, hired Arab labourers. In an interesting parallel he mentioned that the Germans had lost effective control of the Bohemian lands and the Posen area of Poland because of the lack of German labour in these areas and the concentration of the German population in urban, middle-class occupations.[23] Following the admonition of A. D. Gordon, Arlosoroff argued that 'So long as labour in the country is not Jewish, Palestine too, remains Galuth*.'[24]

Arlosoroff did support efforts for the productivization of Jewish life in the Diaspora, but he maintained that such a policy was necessarily of limited scope and ultimately could not succeed because in the Diaspora the Jews did not control the structures of their existence. For all the positive results expected from Jewish consumers' and producers' co-operatives in Eastern Europe in preventing a total and immediate collapse of Jewish existence in those areas, 'without Palestine, the Diaspora cannot be nationally preserved, let alone saved'.[25] Arguing, on the other hand, against the historical determinism of the Zionist Marxists of Poalei Zion, Arlosoroff maintained that such a return to Palestine was not predetermined, nor was it grounded in 'an iron law of necessity or in an economic universal law'. Those who returned to Palestine were not driven or pushed there by economic necessity—in this sense, America was much more powerful: they were moved to Eretz Israel by their will and by their consciousness.

It was this idea of free choice which led Arlosoroff to describe the Zionist pioneer—the *halutz*—as being driven by what appeared to be a combination of Nietzschean will and Lenin's idea of the revolutionary avant-garde. He wrote:

> No, not historical materialism, but a highly-strung national idealism can create these powers in the Jewish

* Exile, or Diaspora

> people that would be strong and capable enough to give rise in Palestine to the pre-conditions of a totally normal and free development of the working Jewish masses.[26]

Only in Palestine could an integral Jewish economic life develop, not limited to the fluctuations of the economic life of other people. Buying land in Palestine—one of the main efforts of the Zionist Organization and the Jewish National Fund—was important, but 'the anchoring of the Jewish people in agricultural life' was even more important. This, Arlosoroff argued, could not, however, be achieved by individual efforts—an overall social vision as well as a national plan were needed for it:

> Palestine will be Jewish only if it is founded on socially healthy and socially just foundations . . . Let Czechoslovaks and Yugoslavs establish their own states according to their own spirit, though we are convinced that even they cannot, in the long run, avoid the demands of a productive, democratic socialism . . . Be this as it may, the Jewish people can rebuild a new homeland only as a true, social cultural community.[27]

If, on the other hand, the Zionist movement decided to build a Jewish Palestine on capitalist foundations, this would lead (a) to a severe limitation of immigration, as very few Jewish capitalists were ready to emigrate to the land; and (b) to a social exploitation of the Arab population. A profit-oriented economy in Palestine, Arlosoroff argued, would have to prefer Arab to Jewish labour and would therefore create a Jewish settler class in the country, not a new national community. A Jewish capitalism in Eretz Israel would not need Jewish workers.

Hence, for Arlosoroff, the single most important policy in the process of the restructuring of the Jewish people in its return to Palestine was the guarantee of public ownership of land. Arlosoroff—like other Zionist socialists—mentioned that the ancient Hebrew traditions of the fallow year and the jubilee were an historical basis which could be utilized on the normative level.[28] This should be accompanied by a number of other institutional arrangements which Arlosoroff saw as crucial both for the success of the enterprise itself—and for its commitment to ideological principles:

> Public ownership of land.
>
> The creation of a national fund for investment. To Arlosoroff, the vital nationalization of production in most European countries during the World War I had proven both the feasibility and efficacy of such a national enterprise, above and beyond the conventional arguments about nationalization between advocates of free enterprise and socialists.[29]
>
> The placing under national control of transit commerce arising from Palestine's geographical position. This was too important to be left to the vagaries of private enterprise.
>
> The launching of a world-wide Jewish loan for Palestine. Given the role of Jewish financiers in raising the war loans of the major European powers during the war, Arlosoroff saw the funds that could be raised through these channels as being more than enough for the infinitely smaller Zionist enterprise.[30]
>
> Extensive encouragement of co-operative societies in Palestine, drawing upon the experience both of Western consumers' and producers' co-operatives as well as some of the more interesting pre-Bolshevik attempts at co-operation in Russia (the Zemstvo movement, etc.).[31]
>
> The introduction of wide-ranging social legislation, regulating working hours, guaranteeing collective bargaining, freedom of association for trade unions, as

well as fixing a maximum price on land in private hands within the Jewish community in Palestine.

## VI

As Arlosoroff's vision of socialism is deeply imbued with cultural values and rooted in historical consciousness, a significant part of his essay on *Jewish People's Socialism* is devoted to cultural matters. Here he starts with the premise that what distinguishes Jewish socialism from other socialist movements is the cultural dimension as much as the socio-economic: if other socialist movements operate within an existing cultural milieu, Jewish socialism, in order to create a socialist Jewish society in Palestine, has to create a Jewish national culture.

Arlosoroff returns time and again to his initial criticism of the European socialist movement for having neglected the cultural dimension in human life: in the Jewish case such a neglect had even more dire consequences. Again, echoes of Russian populism as well as of the German *Zeitgeist* are clearly audible here:

> It is in the working masses that there lives not only a strong social energy, but here also are rooted the founts of the cultural powers of the nation. The working masses are immediately linked to a true, natural, not over-sophisticated and disputatious national cultural sentiment. In their depth there shimmers a spiritual and soulful potential, which has been in chains ever since capitalism killed the soul of the workers . . .
>
> The over-aestheticized, undifferentiated 'culture' which is alienating European nations (and in which so many rootless Jews take part) clearly proves the need of our time for the creative spirit of national life.[32]

Those are strong words, and one can obviously sense how a very dangerous, ethnocentric kind of socialism can be derived from them. But Arlosoroff's further discussion clarifies his meaning with regard to Jewish socialism: it is based on internal reconstruction, on the revival of language, on the socialist commonwealth becoming the keeper of national identity; it is not aggressive towards other national entities. The arguments proposed by Arlosoroff are very similar to those proposed nowadays by socialists among the Catalans, the Basques, the Quebecois and other stateless and oppressed minorities whose very existence is being threatened by a more powerful majority culture:

> The main responsibility of a people's socialism lies in the task of the Jewish working masses to awaken the consciousness of responsibility for the totality of the spiritual development of the nation. It has to educate and develop the cultural consciousness of the people . . . just as capitalism has robbed the working human being of his role in active spiritual and cultural co-operation . . .[33]

The state of Jewish culture, Arlosoroff argued, was paradoxical: on the one hand, it was one of the oldest, if not the oldest, surviving national culture (or—cultural nation: *Kulturnation*); on the other hand, it existed in conditions less developed and more primitive than the culture of the Czechs and the Bulgars. Until there was a Jewish economic infrastructure, controlled by the Jews themselves, a Jewish cultural renaissance could not take place.

It is in this context that Arlosoroff addresses the controversy between 'Hebraists' and 'Yiddishists' (which to a certain degree, but not wholly, was also parallel to the controversy between Zionists and Bundists among Jewish socialists). Arlosoroff comes out clearly and unequivocally—as could be expected—on the side of the 'Hebraists', but his arguments are somewhat novel and original for a socialist.

According to Arlosoroff, the continuity of the historical existence of the Jewish people has been preserved and mediated through the Hebrew language. Hebrew is the language 'which has been born together with the Jewish people. One can even say that it was *through* Hebrew that the Jewish nation was born ... Hebrew has accompanied our people in all its wanderings, within its boundaries the national creations of the Jewish people manifested themselves, even in the Diaspora.'[34] Arlosoroff mentions the Bible, the Talmud, the literature of the Golden Age in Spain, the Kabbalah and Hasidism, the *Haskalah* and the modern Jewish Enlightenment.

In the Palestine of his time, Arlosoroff sees a cultural and linguistic revolution accompanying the Zionist revolution, where Hebrew is being transformed from a language of Jewish high culture to a language of daily intercourse. And it is significant that it was the various Zionist socialist movements—and especially Arlosoroff's own Hapoel Hatzair, with its cultural and ethical approach—which were instrumental in this revival of spoken Hebrew.

Arlosoroff admits that the Jewish masses in Europe do not speak Hebrew but Yiddish, and he acknowledges that the Yiddishists, both the anti-Zionists as well as the Zionists among them, have a strong argument in advocating Yiddish as the 'language of the people'. This, however, to Arlosoroff is not the point: only in a society in which Jews have been economically and socially marginalized—as in Eastern Europe—has this marginalization also been expressed culturally in the creation of a cultural ghetto which effectively shuts Jews off from society at large—*and from their own history*: that was the effect of Yiddish. Just as the twilight economic existence of Jews in the Pale of Settlement (analyzed, as we have seen with cutting insights by Arlosoroff in his treatise) is a proof of their marginality and unproductivity, so Yiddish is also a mark of the Jews being in Exile. As there is no Jewish proletariat in the

Diaspora, he argues, Yiddish cannot be the language of that proletariat. Yiddish is, after all, a language of few cultural achievements—certainly if compared to Hebrew; its cultural nuances cannot be appreciated without a prior knowledge of the cultural Hebrew sources; and, were it to become the only language of the Jews, it would impoverish the multi-dimensionality of Jewish culture and rob the Jews of the richness of their historical heritage, which is stored in Hebrew.[35]

Arlosoroff was scathing in his critique of Yiddish, as were many 'Hebraists' among the Zionists of his generation, and some of his arguments may lack empathy and generosity. Yet his main thesis is simple and valid: an historical renaissance of Jewish life has to be connected with Hebrew. An exclusive link with Yiddish condemns much of the richness of Jewish heritage, and its specific contribution to world culture, to oblivion or incomprehensibility.

In his argument in favour of Hebrew, Arlosoroff brings out the uniqueness of the Jewish socialist revolution in its dialectical relationship to historical continuity. Other socialist movements can revolt against existing reality, since this reality exists. It can be repudiated, because it is already ingrained in human consciousness. Jewish historical reality—be it in the socio-economic or the linguistic and cultural sphere—had been destroyed; hence it could not be simply negated as, for example, French socialists could negate many aspects of French historical memory. The Jewish revolution had to retrieve its own historical reality:

> If the Jewish revolutionary wants to give a true meaning to the Jewish revolution, this can be achieved only through such a restructuring of Jewish life that the unbridgeable gap [*Riss*] in its historical development will be overcome and a new unity emerge from this historical break . . .
>
> It is for this reason that the Jewish revolutionary

> parties have to reconquer and renew Hebrew in the cultural sphere.[36]

In Palestine this could be done only by a culturally conscious working class: the Jewish bourgeoisie, locked in its uncritical admiration for the Enlightenment, could not be the bearer of this transformation. It must start in the Diaspora in what Arlosoroff called 'evolutionary Hebraism'—i.e. through the gradual introduction of Hebrew into the curriculum of Yiddish Jewish schools. When the Jewish masses in Palestine spoke Hebrew, the cultural revolution would spread through the various strata of Jewish society and would not remain the exclusive realm of the intellectuals and writers, as it had been under the *Haskalah*. Hebrew would also become the link between the various communities within Jewish society in Palestine, and its adoption would thus contribute to the restructuring of Jewish society, which was divided linguistically, as well as in so many other ways.

Arlosoroff's essay was a *tour de force*—coming from a young man barely twenty years old: few of the more mature leaders of the Zionist movement at that time were capable of marshalling a comparable array of historical knowledge, theoretical acumen and practical understanding. Bringing his unusual intellectual gifts to his endeavour, he was able—as nobody before him and hardly anyone since—to infuse his discussion of socialist Zionism with a universal meaning. Thus he was able to postulate the Jewish return to labour—and agricultural labour at that—as a paradigm for humanity's transcendence of the alienation imposed on it through sterile mechanization and the urbanization of life under capitalist, bourgeois society. In the same vein, he acknowledged the unique conditions of Jewish socialist transformation as just one example of the socialist movement's transcending its abstract universalism, bequeathed to it by orthodox

Marxism, and evolving a more profound understanding of culture and historical heritage.

Consequently, the emergence of a Jewish socialist society in Palestine could be heralded by Arlosoroff as a model for a new Socialist International, arising, phoenix-like, from the ashes of the Second International so mortally wounded during the 1914-18 War. This new International would not be based on the power of a dictatorship, as the new Third International was about to present itself: by respecting the history and culture of individual nations, this new Socialist International could then justly herald itself as 'the New International of Free Nations'.[37] Within this new socialist world, a niche could also be found for a Jewish socialist society in the historical land of the Jewish people.

# 3
# SOCIALISM AND NATION-BUILDING

## I

After laying down the theoretical foundations of his socialist Zionism in his treatise on *Jewish People's Socialism*, Arlosoroff's interest turned to the more practical policy-oriented problems of Zionism. This was accompanied by his more direct involvement in Zionist activity: it was in the early 1920s that he both emigrated to Palestine and reached a very visible position in his own party, Hapoel Hatzair, as well as in the Zionist Organization.

Yet for all his practical involvement in daily politics, his writings of this period attest to the constant theoretical dimension of his thinking about political issues. One of the major issues addressed by him on this level deals with the major point of difference dividing at that time the bourgeois, middle-class Zionist parties (the so-called General Zionists) from the socialist, left-wing parties within the Zionist movement: should the Jewish settlement of Palestine follow *laissez-faire* economic policies, or should Zionist policies consciously aim at creating a strong public sector in the *Yishuv*? The theoretical debate was also, of course, the expression of a political tug-of-war about control over resources and funds, as well as about the ultimate nature of Jewish society in the Land of Israel: should it be capitalist or socialist?

In the nature of things, this participation in party politics led Arlosoroff to a lot of hectic activity—attending conferences and sitting on committees, both in Palestine and abroad, numerous trips to centres of Zionist activity in Europe and America, and much polemical and ephemeral writing and speaking. We shall, however, deal here mainly with two sets of his writings regarding the future *Yishuv* which bring out the theoretical dimension of Arlosoroff's activity: the first is a lengthy and detailed memorandum written in 1923, on the proposed financial structure of the newly founded Jewish Agency, which was to become the political representative of the Zionist movement in Palestine *vis-à-vis* the British Mandatory authorities; in it Arlosoroff calls for a strong, centralized structure, aiming at ensuring the hegemony of the public sector and the emergence of a social democratic commonwealth in Palestine. The second is a series of articles written in 1925 and immediately afterwards, when a wave of middle-class immigration from Poland ('The Fourth Aliyah') appeared to suggest for the first time that a *laissez-faire* policy, and a middle-class immigration, could prove to be successful and that the *Yishuv* could develop along capitalist lines, and did not have to follow the pioneering and socialist-oriented directions taken by the Second and Third Aliyah. When the capitalist boom of the Fourth Aliyah was reaching its height, Arlosoroff predicted its downfall, and when it crashed, less than two years later, he analyzed in detail what he had considered its necessary shortcomings and then proceeded to argue that only such socially oriented structures as advocated by him in his 1923 memorandum could become an adequate base for the creation of a Jewish national economy in Palestine.

The juxtaposition of his original memorandum with the critical analysis of the Fourth Aliyah provide an unusual example of the relationship between social and economic theory and practical political analysis in Arlosoroff's thinking, with historical reality becoming the practical judge of social theory. In these writings Arlosoroff also emerges as one of the more profound and perceptive thinkers of Zionism, combining an economic and historical understanding (rare among the mostly self-taught left-wing Zionists) with an astute practical understanding of social realities and economic processes as the foundation of political power.

## II

The 1923 memorandum on *The Finances of the Jewish Agency* is an ambitious essay, running to almost 200 pages.[1] It is also a slightly deceptive piece of writing: on the one hand, it appears as a narrow, technical document, trying to lay out, with a lot of financial details, the best way to launch a Jewish world-wide national loan on a massive scale; on the other hand, it is a theoretical piece of social analysis, trying to relate a proposed financial project to social and economic theory and to the ideological debate between the left and the right within the Zionist movement about the socio-economic structure of the *Yishuv*.

As is his custom, Arlosoroff starts with a simple, basic argument: there is no way in which the Zionist enterprise in Palestine could succeed if it were based on individualistic, *laissez-faire* principles. To build a Jewish Palestine on economic theories founded on the profit motive is, to Arlosoroff, utter nonsense: it will not work because it cannot work.

The reasons for this, according to Arlosoroff, are two-fold: firstly, there are reasons embedded in general economic and social development which the advocates of *laissez-faire* Zionism overlook; and, secondly, there are specific reasons which relate to the concrete conditions and contexts of the Zionist enterprise in Palestine.

The attempt to transfer to Palestine the structures of *laissez-faire* private initiative of advanced European societies is, argued Arlosoroff, a grave misconception and it overlooks the fact that even advocates of *laissez-faire* concede that there are a number of crucial functions which in any society have to be undertaken by a public authority. In a developed society, such functions might be of secondary importance; in a society whose economic infrastructures have still to be developed, these functions are central. In a chapter entitled 'The Legend of Private Initiative', Arlosoroff enumerates those functions which can be undertaken only by a public authority:

> Among these there appear all the enterprises and tasks which, in the case of a normal socio-economic development of a nation, have been undertaken over centuries *by society as a whole*: for example, the clearing away of stones and rocks, the draining of swamps, the bringing into cultivation of outlying areas.
>
> These have been historically achieved by various means: in many societies through the co-operative enterprise of large clans of settlers; through the coercive labour of defeated tribes; through the eager devotions of the brethren of ecclesiastical orders, who hacked away at the brush and the undergrowth—or through the hard energies of backwoodsmen: in these various ways roads were laid, land was brought under cultivation, forests were made habitable.[2]

Besides these historical preconditions of opening up a new country for settlement—and the examples brought by Arlosoroff suggest not only settlement in overseas areas, but also the historical examples of development in Europe itself—there are a number of functions which even *laissez-faire* advocates have to admit are carried out in every contemporary society by a public authority:

> Among these are the common needs whose satisfaction, even in civilized societies and in settled areas, is

> excluded from the arbitrary will and the weak powers of the individual and vested in the hands of *the state as such*, as the repository of the general interests of society.
>
> Such interests are the care of the sanitary conditions of the land, the responsibility for public security and, in the most fully developed states also the care for universal education and vocational training of the future generation. Modern internal political life knows the Ministry of Welfare, compulsory education, the modern organization of the police and the militia.[3]

The very nature of such activities implies that large sectors of society and economic life are *by their very nature* outside the scope of private enterprise even according to free market theories. These activities need a public authority. Who would undertake them in Palestine? The British Mandatory Government, according to Arlosoroff, has no interest, inclination or resources for such activities. They would have to be carried out by the Zionist Organization, and this means that these infra-structural activities, a *conditio sine qua non* for the emergence of a Jewish society in Palestine, would have to be undertaken by a Jewish public authority. This Jewish public authority would have to be the Jewish Agency for Palestine, which would thus have to take upon itself a number of quasi-governmental functions: it could not serve as a mere diplomatic intermediary or channel for funds, and hence a private enterprise model could not be followed by the Jewish Agency. A strong, public authority would be needed—a veritable 'state-within-a-state'.

But the transcendence of the capitalist model in the creation of a Jewish society in Palestine was necessary, according to Arlosoroff, also because of the specific Jewish conditions and social structures.

Arlosoroff admits that the Zionist left has no clear policy or theory about how to structure the finances of the Jewish Agency: it knew vaguely what it wanted to achieve—a

Jewish socialist commonwealth in Palestine—but it had no theory tracing the route that such an idea should take in order to become a reality. Arlosoroff attributes the weakness of the Zionist socialists in this respect to a general neglect, on the part of the European socialist movement, of the financial aspects of its programme. Socialist movements usually concentrated on the questions of distribution and consumption, but have traditionally been weaker on questions of production, investment and taxes.[4]

In the history of the *Yishuv*, the workers had been, according to Arlosoroff, the vanguard of the Jewish settlement effort in Palestine, and the socialist parties had become gradually but steadily stronger and more important in the structure of the Zionist movement as the Zionist enterprise moved from ideological debate and propaganda in the Diaspora to the praxis of 'claiming the land' in Zion. Basic tenets of socialist Zionism—the principle of Jewish labour and the public ownership of land—had gradually become universally recognized within the Zionist movement. But in order to guarantee that these achievements would be firmly institutionalized, much more had to be done.

In this context Arlosoroff takes to task those within the Zionist movement who spend enormous amounts of time trying to gain from the British Government—and the League of Nations, responsible for the Mandate for Palestine—a clearer and legally more binding definition of the powers of the Jewish Agency and the responsibilities of the British Government with regard to the Jewish National Home clauses of the Mandate. Those circles who saw this as the most important task of Zionism—and they were mostly on the right—were, according to Arlosoroff, mistaken and wasting their time. It is precisely the ambiguity of some of the legislation surrounding the Jewish Agency which gave it ample room to manoeuvre in those 'grey zones', and it was not legal formulae, but actual economic and social activity which would determine the future of the Zionist enterprise,

Arlosoroff argued in one of the classical instances of the presentation of his 'constructivist' approach to Zionism:

> The 'National Home', as well as its instrument, the Jewish Agency, will become in the world of reality what we will make them to be . . . This means, first of all, that what they will become depends on the economic and social energies that we shall succeed in pouring into their juridical forms.[5]

The question was not what would be the legal *status* of the newly founded Jewish Agency, but what would be its *functions*, Arlosoroff argued in a formula which was to become almost a principle of socialist Zionism. And according to him, it would have to be primarily an organ planning and carrying out immigration and settlement policy, financing these and creating the economic and social conditions for their success.

Arlosoroff goes on to argue both against the extreme left wing of the socialist Zionist movement as well as against the *laissez-faire* General Zionists—that in an ideal world planning should start from desiderata; but in the actual world of cruel reality, Zionist planning had to start from an extremely disadvantageous situation—the chaos of post-World War I Europe. Zionism has to start, Arlosoroff writes,

> . . . from the destructive, anarchically developing forces, which have been unleashed by the imperialist war . . . The various national economies have been destroyed and impoverished, the economic relations between the nations have been either fundamentally brought to a standstill or arbitrarily discontinued . . . The process of class warfare in the capitalist societies, which has been radicalized extraordinarily due to the world economic crisis, causes a revolutionary disrup-

> tion of social ties and a rapid progress of social decomposition.[6]

Under such conditions, the Zionist movement cannot hark back to the harmonistic platitudes of pre-1914 free-market theories, much as Zionism, as a movement of national reconstruction, would have preferred 'a quiet and clear atmosphere, stable conditions of life and a world of assured safe values'.[7] Under the unsettled conditions of such a chaotic world, to expect individual Jews to migrate to Palestine of their own accord and in their own good time, and attempt there, by individual trial and error and the corrective forces of the market, to establish for themselves a new existence in the new land, would tend to be suicidal. The low number of Jewish immigrants to Palestine during 1922-23 is for Arlosoroff a proof of this. Alternative ideas, about the Land of Israel as a spiritual centre for the Jewish people (Ahad Ha'am's ideas, for example, for whose moral sensitivities Arlosoroff had much sympathy) would still be meaningless without the basis of a large, extensive and economically viable Jewish population in Palestine.[8]

Individual settlement on the land would not succeed, Arlosoroff argued, and an urban Jewish population would need the hinterland of a planned Jewish agricultural economy. The lack of natural resources in Palestine made planning even more imperative. Private capital would come 'only if it could be lured by the availability of cheap labour, and this in the conditions of Palestine meant "native", i.e. non-Jewish, labour'.[9] Historically, for this reason, private investments were traditionally unsuccessful in Palestine: only national and philanthropic enterprises have succeeded under these conditions.

To those Zionists who feared the socialist implications of Arlosoroff's conditions and opposed them for ideological reasons,[10] he pointed out that economic and political developments during World War I had radically transformed, due to munitions industries and huge national loans, the most fundamental structures of the European world. All European societies possessed much more centralized economies, and a small country like Palestine would find it difficult to compete on a *laissez-faire* model with much larger, virtually nationalized European economies.[11] Furthermore,

> Those Zionists who wish to realize our settlement and its finances through methods and means which were feasible 250 years ago in the age of the Pilgrim Fathers, or even a hundred years ago during the Westward drive, belong in a museum, if not in the department of the Bronze Age and spinning wheel, at least alongside Stephenson's locomotive and Sir Walter Raleigh's tobacco pipe.[12]

After making the allusion to the European colonial experience, Arlosoroff does however insist that from a purely economic point of view, the Jewish settlement in Palestine is totally different—and hence attempting to draw parallels would be misleading: contrary to the European colonial experience, in the case of Palestine, the land itself which is to be settled is not of any appreciable economic value, nor has the specific territory—Palestine—been chosen for economic reasons as the most profitable or potentially bountiful land. The choice was determined by considerations transcending economics—historical memory, national identity—and consequently the means required to carry out such a project cannot be articulated in purely economic terms.[13]

The only way to achieve the necessary capital to launch the massive settlement necessary to create a Jewish infrastructure in the land would be, according to Arlosoroff, through a world-wide Jewish national loan, and he devoted the bulk of his memorandum to an attempt to prove that such a project was economically feasible and that a campaign to launch such a loan was not a wild pipe dream. Yet, to Arlosoroff, the meaning of such a loan (at the going rate of $4\frac{1}{2}$%) went beyond its mere economic dimension: its very existence would create a world-wide network of Jewish solidarity, involving masses of Jews who would never have dreamt of going to Palestine themselves but would thus be connected with the national effort of settling the Jewish homeland. This would also bring about the required combination of public finance and working-class, co-operative settlement which, given the non-existence of a Jewish sovereign power, would be the parallel to what in any other nation would be a socialist policy linking public funds to the working class. Such a policy would be an adequate expression of the idea of self-help and the auto-emancipation of the Jewish popular masses who were fighting for their freedom, carried out into the field of capital-formation for national purposes.[14] It was this link between the social and national aspect of the Jewish revolution which could thus become the instrument of creating the basis of actual Jewish economic and political power in Palestine:

> The essence of our endeavour does not extend to organizing a state apparatus or to inaugurating a machinery of government; luckily, we do not have to equip an army or paint fortifications in blue-and-white. We bear, however, the much more difficult task of creating an integrated society on our land, of bringing about the emergence of a settled, active population in a country with productive conditions of life, of laying the foundations of our national economy as well as of our national culture.[15]

The ambitiousness of Arlosoroff's plan becomes clear when he spells out the functions he sees the Jewish Agency taking upon itself through the massive, world-wide Jewish loan:

—The purchase of land and the initial investment in preparing it for cultivation.
—The distribution of loans for co-operative settlements.
—The distribution of loans for urban construction.
—The setting up of credit for imports and raw materials.
—The creation of a note-issuing bank, parallel to that of the government. The issuing of such a Zionist currency, convertible to the Egyptian pound then used as legal tender in Palestine, would give the Jewish Agency greater control over its own budget by actually issuing its own currency.[16]

Arlosoroff's plan was truly ambitious, and the Jewish Agency as constituted had to settle for a much more modest set of goals. The idea of a world-wide Jewish loan—or a voluntary tax—was only to be realized much later, under the twin pressures of the Holocaust in Europe and the establishment of an independent State of Israel. Yet the *public* nature of the Jewish settlement of the Land of Israel did follow Arlosoroff's prognosis that the Zionist revolution could not be carried out by individual settlers on a free market basis. Development in Palestine bore out Arlosoroff's contention that the Jewish Agency would, through its economic activity, lay the infrastructure for a Jewish society and eventually a Jewish polity in Palestine. The Jews would become a political factor in Palestine, Arlosoroff argued, only if they were economically strong and self-sufficient in the country. This would also have to be a deterrent to the incipient tendency of the *Yishuv* to live beyond its means—an issue to be taken up with gusto by Arlosoroff in his biting critique of the conspicuous consumption of the Fourth Aliyah. Arlosoroff's 'constructivist' approach is best expressed in his own summing up, when he says that only if the Jewish *Yishuv* became economically dominant in Palestine would it have a chance of political victory:

> Neither by claims of historical rights, nor by diplomatic efforts, certainly not by military might or even

> numerical superiority, can the Jewish people succeed in its national war of liberation in Palestine. This can be achieved only through the hard and constant energy of settlement and economic reconstruction [*Aufbau*], which will strike roots for all eternity in the soil of our land for the community of Jewish workers and settlers.[17]

## III

During the years 1924-25, in the wake of a political campaign launched by a nationalistic Polish Government aimed at 'polonizing' trade and commerce, a wave of middle-class Polish Jewish immigrants reached Palestine. Had the gates of the United States not been closed at that time to Eastern European Jews because of the recently enacted American racist immigration laws, it is conceivable that many of these newcomers would have preferred to follow earlier Jewish waves of immigration in pursuit of the American Dream. As it was, they ended up in Eretz Israel.

This 'Fourth Aliyah' (also colloquially referred to as 'Grabski's Aliyah', after the Polish Minister of Finance who initiated the policy of trying to squeeze Jews out of urban commerce), brought to Palestine for the first time a sizeable number of immigrants who were not imbued with, or motivated by, pioneering ideals: nor were they in any way touched by a socialist vision of a new, fundamentally different society in the Land of Israel. For the first time a mass of Jews reached Eretz Israel wanting not to transform their lives—to become peasants, workers, pioneers, communist redeemers of their nation and of the world in general—but only wishing to continue, under conditions of freedom for themselves as Jews, their previous modes of existence and their former occupations. They did not settle on the land, they had no burning urge to become agricultural workers, nor did they join kibbutzim or try out new forms of social organization. Many of them brought some money with them and came with their families—very different from the *halutzim* who were for the most part young and single—and set themselves up in business, mainly in Tel Aviv.

The infusion of this money and this kind of immigration into the small, economically underdeveloped *Yishuv*, created an unprecedented economic boom, especially in construction, and contributed to the rapid growth of Tel Aviv: those areas of central Tel Aviv, especially around Allenby, Ahad Ha'am and Nachlat Binyamin Streets, which remind the discerning visitor of certain areas of Warsaw, Lodz and Bialystok, date back to this period.

On the political level, this middle-class immigration, which transferred to Palestine the economic activity of Eastern European Jewry with its mercantile ethos, appeared to suggest that what had by then emerged as a Zionist truism—i.e., that Eretz Israel could be built mainly by pioneers and under the banner of socialist Zionism—seemed to have been overtaken by events. A middle-class market-oriented economy could also flourish in Palestine, and Zionist capitalism appeared to have a bright future: not all roads to Zion necessarily led to a socialist-oriented society.

Such a development also appeared to contradict the basic premises and political consequences of Arlosoroff's own theoretical writings, both in his *Jewish People's Socialism* and in his memorandum on the finances of the Jewish Agency. Arlosoroff responded to this challenge both during the apparent success of the Fourth Aliyah as well as after its débâcle. In both instances, his insights merit close scrutiny.

Arlosoroff's 1925 article *On the Structure of the Fourth Aliyah* opens with a frank acknowledgement of its obvious achievements: it raised dramatically the number of immigrants to Palestine, developed whole areas of the country, especially in Tel Aviv and a few other urban centres, and gave a significant push to commercial activity. Yet it also caused a steep rise in prices, caused rents to sky-rocket and brought about a wave of hectic land speculation. It also introduced into Palestinian provincialism a little bit of elegance ('according to Warsaw's latest fashion', Arlosoroff could not help himself from quipping). It energized the *Yishuv*, uplifted the spirit of the Jewish inhabitants of the country, and instilled new hopes into the rather stagnant back-water reality of Jewish life in Eretz Israel.[18]

Yet Arlosoroff views this unprecedented prosperity with caution: is it truly contributing to the productive capacity of the *Yishuv*—or is it merely an ephemeral speculative boom, doomed to be necessarily followed by a crash? Regardless of the obvious satisfaction every Zionist should feel at the spectacle of more Jews coming to Palestine, Arlosoroff could not refrain from asking 'what is [this Aliyah's] worth from the point of view of political economy and society? What does it contribute to our settlement effort as measured by [our] national, economic and political aims?'[19]

Arlosoroff was aware that the eighteen months from the beginning of the Fourth Aliyah in 1924 was too short a time to pass definite judgement, yet major tendencies could, according to him, already be discerned. It was these which Arlosoroff set out to analyze coolly and dispassionately, beyond the emotional and ideological polemics between the Zionist left and right.

Arlosoroff's first point is to observe that most of the new immigrants of the Fourth Aliyah are settling in the urban areas—and primarily in Tel Aviv. Some of the immigrants are ready to settle on the land, but 'the dominant social typology of most of the immigrants, and the conditions of their development are directly connected with the city, with city life and urban occupations ... This urban tendency characterized by the new immigration has also contributed to a hypertrophy in this direction ...'[20]

Arlosoroff cites a few figures to underline the structural meaning of these sociological changes caused by the Fourth Aliyah: at the end of the war, the agricultural population made up 15.4% of the total Jewish population of Palestine; the pioneering Third Aliyah immediately after the war raised this population to 18.1%. Since the beginning of the Fourth Aliyah, the ratio of the agricultural population rapidly declined—to 15.7% at the end of 1924 and to 14.4% on 1 May, 1925—and it continued to go down.[21] Even those who settled in the *moshavot*—the established agricultural settlements of the private sector—became merchants, real estate brokers and commercial agents rather than farmers. More than two-thirds of the new immigrants settled in Tel Aviv, thus dramatically contributing to the imbalance between the Jewish urban sector and its agricultural hinterland.

A further breakdown of the occupational structures of the new immigrants who settled in Tel Aviv showed, according to Arlosoroff, that the main increase occurred in commercial and not industrial occupations. In another study of the Fourth Aliyah, published at the same time, Arlosoroff showed that while the number of industrial enterprises in Tel Aviv rose in 1923-24 by 31.1% and that of workshops by 24.7%, the number of offices rose by 96.8%. Of the population growth of Tel Aviv during 1925-26 of more than 13,000, only 2,098 were absorbed in industry, manufacture and other productive occupations.[22]

These and other figures, as well as the emergence of the traditional Jewish *Luftmensch*—that demi-monde denizen of unspecified Jewish commercial life, not doing anything in particular but living off the bits and pieces of marginal deals—led Arlosoroff to the conclusion that the Diaspora was being re-established in the Land of Israel:

> Does this not mean that we are renewing the economic structures known to us from the countries of the Jewish Galuth—that inverted social pyramid, perched on its narrow tip and in danger of being upset by every wind and by anyone's ten fingers? How could there emerge,

> on such a basis, a self-sustaining National Home, a Jewish commonwealth?[23]

Arlosoroff points out that his strictures against Tel Aviv's centrality in the Fourth Aliyah should not be interpreted as an uncritical, romantic anti-industrialism. Of course the world had known great commercial urban centres like Liverpool and Rotterdam, which had developed as major centres of world trade. But, he added, 'one does not have to enlarge on the difference between Liverpool or Rotterdam and Tel Aviv: it is the same difference as that between Liverpool and Pinsk, between Rotterdam and Kalisch'.[24] Tel Aviv was in danger of becoming not a centre of a newly structured Jewish society, but just another Jewish immigrants' community, without a productive base. It is a recognizable picture:

> It is the picture that Jewish immigration produces anywhere and everywhere within capitalist society. London's Whitechapel, New York's East Side, the Jewish areas of Buenos Aires and Johannesburg are only the milestones of the last decades on this way. On Palestinian soil, the same social and economic law will apply as on Polish, Argentinian or South African soil.[25]

It was not only that most immigrants gravitated towards Tel Aviv, but that within Tel Aviv itself they congregated in Diaspora-type occupations, 'there emerges in our cities a massive concentration of people who are nothing [more] than a lowly proletariat of petty-merchants and small artisans, socially and economically oppressed, irrational and costly from the vantage point of political economy. Without real welfare, without healthy conditions of life, without economic perspectives.'[26]

Moreover, such an urban growth, unaccompanied by a parallel growth in the Jewish agricultural sector, would create a growing society of consumers of agricultural goods.

The outcome would be, paradoxically, that this development of the Jewish urban population would strengthen the growth of the *Arab* agricultural sector, as the Jewish 'urban islands' around Tel Aviv created a demand for agricultural products which could be supplied only by Arab farmers.[27] We shall later see that Arlosoroff was one of the more far-sighted Zionist thinkers and leaders in his sensitivity to the emergence of a Palestinian-Arab national movement: yet this attitude did not preclude him from seeing the absurdity—and the eventual dangerous consequences for a Jewish national renaissance—of the spectacle of a rootless, urban Jewish population in Palestine helping to bolster up Arab agricultural development of the land.

Arlosoroff's understanding of the economic basis of political life moved him to warn not only that the Fourth Aliyah speculative boom would be short-lived, but that the very structure of this Aliyah posed in itself a danger to the Zionist enterprise. It created an illusion of a growing Jewish population which did not, however, control the destiny of the country:

> It is not he who controls Tel Aviv, Bat Galim or Beth Hakerem*—even with tens of thousands of inhabitants—who will determine the political and economic future of the country. Not even he who possesses the concession for the Port of Haifa or the waterworks of the Jordan: it will be determined by those who on the Plain of Acre hold the plough in their hands and by those whose fields will be irrigated by these water canals.[28]

Palestine, as part of the Levant, was, Arlosoroff argued, in a stationary economic state: economic development could be introduced only by the dynamic, transformative impetus of a

* Jewish garden suburbs of Haifa and Jerusalem, respectively.

pioneering Jewish immigration which would create, through its collective social power—as envisaged by Arlosoroff in his earlier writings—the infrastructure for change. Petty commercial and mercantile activities, as then exemplified by land speculation in Tel Aviv, could in any case be performed in the Levant with even greater distinction by 'Arabs, Armenians and Greeks'.[29] What appeared to many Zionists as a new beginning, Arlosoroff foresaw as a bubble—and a dangerous illusion.

Within a year of the publication of Arlosoroff's article, his doubts were fully vindicated, and a major economic crisis engulfed the *Yishuv*, accompanied by unemployment, bankruptcies and massive emigration. In 1926 Arlosoroff analyzed this in an essay on *The Economic Conditions of the Yishuv*.[30] But his more extensive and detailed account of what went wrong—and why it *had* to go wrong—did not appear until 1928, in *Consequences*.[31]

On the one hand Arlosoroff had the doubtless advantage of having warned against the phoney prosperity of the Fourth Aliyah while it lasted. On the other hand, as a Zionist leader he also had to engage in political damage control, lest the post-Fourth Aliyah crisis turned into a general rout of the Zionist enterprise and would be viewed as such by Jews, Arabs—and the British Administration. For this reason he pointed out in *Consequences* that the crisis was a very specific one, rooted in the unusual social composition of the Fourth Aliyah—and was *not* a structural crisis of Zionism, nor should it be attributed to faulty policies of the Zionist Executive or the non-co-operation of the socialist wing in the Zionist movement, which might have feared the success of a middle-class aliyah.[32]

Arlosoroff tries to go beyond platitudes or ideology to the bare economic facts: the Fourth Aliyah showed that even immigrants coming with their own capital needed direction and could not, in the conditions of Palestine, be left to their own devices and the mercy of the market place. The structure of the Fourth Aliyah—middle-class families as against the single, young *halutzim* of former immigrations—created its own problems: while young unattached pioneers, going out to settle the land, had a low level of expectations as well as of actual consumption, and become involved in production from an early stage, the typical Fourth Aliyah immigrants were in fact a burden to the economy:

> The lack of a financial basis made itself felt even more, because the middle-class aliyah brought to the country families with many children and a relatively higher standard of living. Since their integration did not occur without difficulties and took some time, it turned out that a large part of the capital brought by these families was used for their immediate needs.[33]

Although a large amount of the imported capital was invested in machinery and raw materials, even in those (few) cases where a serious attempt at production was made, very little was left as business capital, and hence the chances of success were minimal.[34]

But the main problem of the Fourth Aliyah remained its internal imbalance between high consumption and low productivity. A small and poor country like Palestine—and the small Jewish *Yishuv* within it—could not then afford, Arlosoroff argued, European standards of living at a time when the economic infrastructures of society had not yet been established. The middle-class Fourth Aliyah introduced unheard of demands into Palestinian-Jewish society which could not be sustained by the local, Jewish economy:

> Our urban *Yishuv*—wearing English cloth, consuming German chocolate, Arab vegetables, Australian butter and Romanian flour—cannot justify the high expenditures of its standard of living by charging high prices for its products . . .

> [This imbalance between consumption and production] has to be redressed if we do not want to be transformed into another society living on alms [= *Haluka*, i.e. the system of contributions which sustained the old, Orthodox pre-Zionist Jewish community in Palestine] . . .[35]

The boom of the Fourth Aliyah was accompanied by all the characteristic traits of land speculation, rapid construction and credit—all fuelled by the high standards of living of the new, middle-class immigrants. Arlosoroff quotes an American Zionist leader who said that American Zionists, as against Palestinian-Jewish socialists, did not see a lower standard of living as an ideal. Arlosoroff agreed—he saw no virtue in poverty, asceticism and deprivation as such: but the low standard of living of the *halutzim* in Palestine was crucial for capital formation. It was equivalent to that stage of early European industrialization which created the conditions of economic development:

> Palestinian-Jewish workers do not see a low standard of living as an ideal. On the contrary, their ideal is to create, according to what is possible, higher and more dignified living conditions for every labouring human being. But what distinguishes a worker in Palestine from a Zionist leader is his determination to strike roots in the land under the conditions of Palestinian reality as well as his realization of an iron-like coercion which forces him to create a certain balance between the possibilities of production and his own needs.[36]

According to Arlosoroff, such conscious self-denial can be inculcated in highly motivated members of élitist political movements, especially if they are young and single—the members of the pioneering youth organization and socialist Zionist movements. It cannot work among middle-class families fleeing commercial discrimination in Poland, whose only wish—legitimate and understandable as it may be—is to re-establish for themselves in Tel Aviv their former occupations, their standards of living as well as the life styles to which they have been accustomed in Warsaw or Bialystok. Such goals were unattainable in Palestine then, and the attempt to achieve them was counter-productive from the point of view of the Zionist enterprise. Like every revolution, Zionism had to go through a harsh period—but in the Zionist case, Arlosoroff argued, this should not be based on coercion or class domination, but on a hard-won idealism:

> We do not intend to be guests coming for a cure to a resort: we have to deal with settling the land. It is with this in mind that we came to this country of poor *fellahin*,* whose population lives in misery, whose soil is meagre and exhausted, a country that does not have natural resources and possesses no developed market and no significant urban industry. And to this land we bring European standards of living![37]

Arlosoroff warns that the conventional Jewish milieu lacks the kind of puritan tradition which was so instrumental in European and American industrialization (and which in the Australian case was substituted by the conditions of the penal settlement of the continent). Eventually, according to Arlosoroff, the Land of Israel would be civilized and cultured: but he was concerned that the Fourth Aliyah had created in Palestine an inordinate taste for higher education, as if all the children could become 'academics, virtuosi and artists'. He saw the *embourgeoisement* of life in Palestine, due to the Fourth Aliyah, as pernicious:

> Through Warsaw fashions, living conditions of the Russian-Jewish bourgeoisie, evening performances,

* Arab peasants

> concerts, theatre and other such 'little things' we have raised our standard of living to a degree where it stands in dire contrast to the productive forces of the country . . .[38]

As a consequence of the experience of the Fourth Aliyah Arlosoroff called for a conscious educational effort to curb the drive for higher standards of living in Palestine. He knew such a call would encounter a sceptical reaction: he none the less saw it as crucial for the formation of a new society.

The major issue, however, remained the same: the productivization and industrialization of the country, and this could be done only 'through national and public capital',[39] not through the efforts of individual immigrants coming with their little bit of money. He called for the Jewish Agency to extend loans to failing businessmen of the Fourth Aliyah, provided they were ready to move into production. Other families should be helped, from national funds, to settle on the land: Arlosoroff was worried that Jews were speculatively buying land from Arabs, then building apartments (which in many cases remained unoccupied), whilst the Arab land-owner was investing his money in citrus groves.[40] Coming back to his ambitious plans for nationally financed industries, Arlosoroff hoped that the Zionist Executive would at least settle for a more intensive system of financing industries from national resources. Private enterprise—so the Fourth Aliyah had shown according to Arlosoroff—could not build an economy in the conditions of Palestine: neither could it build a nation. For this, an overall social policy was necessary. Nation building and social reconstruction go together, and the Fourth Aliyah experience was to Arlosoroff a living proof that this was not merely a theoretical scheme: reality had proved it as the only feasible way for nation-building.

# 4
# BETWEEN JEW AND ARAB

## I

It took the Zionist movement some time to realize that the very processes which helped establish the Jewish community in the Land of Israel as a national entity were also bringing about the emergence of an Arab national movement in the country and that both movements were dialectically related to each other.[1] While there had been isolated Zionist thinkers before him—notably Ahad Ha'am and Yitzhak Epstein—who expressed similar views, Arlosoroff was one of the first Zionist leaders to recognize the fact that Zionism was facing a Palestinian-Arab national movement. It was his historical and sociological knowledge which added an extra edge to this realization. Because Arlosoroff's Zionism was anchored in a set of universalist principles, and was not just an expression of Jewish agony, it was easier for him to address the issue. Most Zionist leaders—and this includes many within the socialist Zionist parties—reacted to Arab opposition to the Zionist enterprise emotionally and with highly charged ethnocentric self-righteousness. Nor were many of them intellectually equipped to deal with the issue adequately, and the sometimes murderous manifestations of Arab nationalism in Palestine made—and still make—such a dispassionate discourse difficult.

The first reference in Arlosoroff's works to the Arabs of

Palestine appears, almost as an afterthought, in his treatise on *Jewish People's Socialism*: when insisting on the necessity of basing the Jewish settlement effort on Jewish labour, Arlosoroff goes on, however, to admit that the Arab problem is 'extremely complex' and should be 'justly dealt with'. Then he adds that 'a future Jewish Palestine will guarantee every *fellah* his full freedom and the autonomous regulation of his national-cultural and national-social needs'.[2] Though couched in generalities, this reference still suggests that even at this early stage, and before his first visit to Palestine, Arlosoroff was aware of the national dimension of the problem: it was not just a problem of individual rights, but of national identity.

But Arlosoroff's first detailed attempt at comprehending the problem did not appear until 1921. In the wake of the Arab anti-Jewish riots of 1921—the first major disturbances under British rule in Palestine—Arlosoroff, who was in the country on his first extended visit, tried to address the problem at a level both novel and courageous in the context of the Zionist movement. Few at that time proved to be as far-sighted.

In 'The Events of May' (1921), Arlosoroff clearly states that the Zionist movement has to realize that it is confronted by a national movement on the part of the Palestinian Arabs. He criticizes Zionist leaders, and even some whom he mockingly calls 'moderate socialists', who called for tougher and more repressive police measures against the Arab rioters and hoped that such a law-and-order approach could solve the problem. This, according to Arlosoroff, is to misjudge the issue. Whilst those rioters who are guilty of murder and pillage should, of course, be dealt with all the severity of the law

> The question of our political relationship with the Arab people living in Palestine, and particularly the question of the nature of the Arab movement, are not questions

> to be settled by the criminal code or by our present anger at the spilled blood. These are questions about the forms of our life in the country, which will be common to us and to them for all eternity.[3]

The question is a political one and must be addressed as such, and not relegated to merely ethnological or sociological explanations. To Arlosoroff the problem is a simple one: 'Does there exist an Arab national movement in the country, and what is its nature?' He replies unequivocally:

> Yes, there exists such a force. Let us not fool ourselves: there does exist in the country a national mass united by Arab slogans; whether we call it a national movement or not—we have to understand its nature and determine our attitudes towards it.[4]

Arlosoroff admits that by European standards, Palestinian-Arab nationalism may not possess all the qualities and attributes associated with a fully-fledged national movement: 'If we consider the economic and social conditions on whose basis there emerged Italian, Polish or even Jewish nationalism ... we may apparently reach the judgement that there does not exist here an Arab national movement, nor is there any possibility for such a movement to emerge within the conditions of Arab society.'[5] But such a judgement would be an attempt to 'conduct an ostrich-like policy'.[6]

It is true, Arlosoroff further admits, that compared to European conditions, economic activity among Palestinian Arabs is very primitive and rudimentary, and many Arabs are still semi-nomads; commerce is limited, and industry is virtually non-existent; early capitalist development—which in such non-European countries as Japan, Egypt and India has contributed to the emergence of a unified national consciousness—has not yet occurred among Palestinian

Arabs; Bedouins and *fellahin* are set against each other, as are Christians and Muslims; social life still revolves around the *khamula*, the clan; the level of education is low, etc. etc.

Yet despite all this, anyone denying the existence of an Arab national movement among Palestinian Arabs because its characteristics are different from the standard European experience is 'like a doctor who denies the existence of a malady in an obviously sick person because the microbes he finds in the blood of the patient are different from those he is used to seeing under the microscope'.[7] Moreover, Arlosoroff argues against those in the Zionist movement who claim 'outside agitators' were responsible for encouraging the riots. To Arlosoroff it does not matter whether non-Palestinian Arab activists, agents of European powers or some absentee Arab land-owners helped to fuel the riots: the point is that they did succeed in what they set out to do because of the response of the Palestinian Arabs, and hence

> An Arab movement does exist. It would be pernicious for us to belittle it, or to rely on bayonets, be they Jewish or English, to suppress it. You can rely on bayonets only for a limited period of time, but not for decades.[8]

The existence of an Arab national movement is to Arlosoroff a function of its ability to move and command concerted social action. Compared to the level of organization of the Arabs in Palestine when the British conquered the country in 1917, by 1921 Palestinian Arabs had made significant progress. He argues that one cannot but be impressed by the efficacy of organization within the Arab community:

> During these weeks we have witnessed—following the events in Jaffa—a number of developments: the activities on the part of the Arabs have been surprisingly well organized and have been carried out successfully. One

> example: seven Arabs are accused and imprisoned by the authorities—and the Arabs of Jaffa carry out an organized protest, all merchants close their shops, organize a demonstration in front of Government House and send a delegation calling for the release of the prisoners.[9]

All this, as well as the Arab economic boycott of Jewish commerce, are to Arlosoroff clear and uncontestable proof that an effective national movement exists among the Palestinian Arabs. What, then, should the Zionist response be?

It should be neither a denial of the existence of such an Arab national movement, nor an emotional call for 'tough measures'. His conclusion is unequivocal—just as is his statement that a Palestinian Arab national movement does exist:

> We have only one way—the way of peace, and only one policy—the policy of mutual understanding. It is especially important to say these things now, in a moment of rage and anger ... Because of existing conditions, Jews and Arabs are pushed into one path, and therefore they are in need of the politics of compromise ...
>
> One quick look at the European history of states and nations would teach us this: whenever two powerful vital interests clash—there is only one way out: a mutual compromise.[10]

Arlosoroff has no illusions: such a policy of compromise will not emerge overnight, nor will it be brought about by a quick British willingness to cave in before Arab riots. He is also adamant in maintaining that a policy of peace and compromise on the Jewish side should not be mistaken for a policy of weakness or self-liquidation. On the contrary:

> The Arabs, too, will have to understand that they have no other way except the politics of peace, that the determination of the Hebrew nation to build its national home in Eretz Israel is irrevocable. They should know that the more this land is soaked with Jewish blood, the more obstinate will be our will to strike roots in it.[11]

Acknowledging the existence of Palestinian-Arab nationalism does not mean, to Arlosoroff, abandoning Zionism: compromise built on strength is Arlosoroff's policy, and this means a constant attempt to reach out to the Arab population and convince them that they too have to acknowledge the existence of a Jewish national movement. Compromise is a two-way process. From the Zionist perspective, however, neither seeking confrontation, nor a sterile attempt to deny the very existence—or legitimacy—of Arab nationalism in Palestine should be the policy pursued. Looking for compromise and co-existence appears to Arlosoroff to be the only way which can create the conditions that are necessary for the continued Jewish effort in Palestine.

This approach, influenced by Arlosoroff's wider humanistic concerns, but rooted in a hardy realism, appears again two years later in his memorandum on the finances of the Jewish Agency:

> In Palestine itself the development of the Arab population has reached in certain aspects a new stage. The last years have brought about the beginning of a yet underdeveloped but rapidly progressing growth in the emergence of a national movement. Even if there might be differences in the assessment of its actual power, its significant latent forces cannot basically be denied.[12]

Few Zionists were ready to make this admission in 1921 or 1923.

## II

If this was Arlosoroff's view at the beginning of the clashes between Arabs and Jews in the early 1920s (which soon blew over, though they left a deep impact on the consciousness of both sides), the much more violent disturbances of 1929, which led to many deaths, severely tested his willingness to pursue a policy of compromise. This was compounded by the changed political circumstances—primarily due to the emergence of a militant right-wing movement within Zionism. This movement, organized by Jabotinsky through his Union of Revisionist Zionists and its brown-shirted youth movement Betar, by then articulated much more aggressive anti-Arab attitudes than those existing in the early twenties.

When discussing the 1929 riots—which spread from Jerusalem to Hebron, Jaffa and Safed—it should be mentioned that these Arab disturbances broke out in a politically and religiously explosive atmosphere within whose context there occurred a number of Jewish attempts, initiated mainly by the Betar youth movement, to maintain, enhance and enlarge, if necessary by force, Jewish rights around the Wailing Wall. These rights were severely curtailed by a timid British policy of maintaining a fragile *status quo*, and Betar consciously chose to challenge it. While none of these attempts by Betar members could even remotely justify the wanton killing, by Arab gangs, of dozens of innocent and defenceless Jewish civilians, including women and children, and the indiscriminate massacres of entire Jewish communities—such as the ultra-Orthodox, non-Zionist community in Hebron—the political context of the outbreak of violence should not be overlooked. After the riots broke out the *Yishuv* obviously united to preserve Jewish lives; but the developments leading to the outbreak of the violence witnessed some very deep and fundamental divisions between the moderate Zionist establishment, of which Arlosoroff was by then already a prominent member, which tried to follow the constructivist and non-confrontational policies advocated by Arlosoroff himself in 1921—and the consciously aggressive policies of Betar which focused on such areas rich in symbolism—and violent potential—as the Wailing Wall and the Temple Mount. It is the irony of history that the political debate in Israel in the 1980s repeats these two different approaches.

Arlosoroff's first spontaneous response to the riots is indicative of his later, more analytical assessment. He was in London for a Zionist Executive meeting when the riots occurred, and his first response can be gleaned from a letter written to his wife from London on first hearing the news about the riots and the Jewish victims killed. Expressing his shock and dismay at the slaughter of defenceless Jewish families by Arab gangs, Arlosoroff is not swept away by righteous indignation, but goes on to criticize the ill-advised attempts of the Revisionists to focus attention on the explosive issue of the Wailing Wall, so sensitive to the Arabs and Muslims because of its proximity to the mosques on the Temple Mount. Referring to the narrow alley leading then (and until 1967) to the Wailing Wall, Arlosoroff wrote:

> What is all this excitement about? What good does it do? This damned [*verfluchte*] entrance to the Wailing Wall is truly a cul-de-sac, which will cost us most dearly. Blood, quiet, nerves, goodwill, constructive ability, relations and contacts that are hard to maintain, the security of our brethren—all this will be the price we will have to pay for it.[13]

In a detailed report written later in 1929 (*Attempt at a Summing-Up*) Arlosoroff followed the same reasoning, which condemns what he calls 'the Revisionist provocation' as both immoral and imprudent. Despite the murderousness of the Arab gangs, Arlosoroff reiterated what had been his approach since 1921: that there existed an Arab national movement in Palestine and that Zionist policies could not be oblivious of this fact. He quoted his own statements to that effect from 1921 and argued that since then this Arab national movement had undergone further development along the following lines:[14]

> Education: 'the most important of these factors is the continuing and relatively important progress of Arab primary education . . . staffed by teachers, the majority of whom are imbued with Arab fighting spirit'. Youth organizations, like the YMCA and other institutions affiliated with American and British missionaries, helped in fostering this national consciousness especially among Christian Arabs.
>
> The modernization of Arab society, paradoxically hastened by developments introduced by Jewish immigration. This includes integrative communications between the various sectors of Arab society: 'One can assume that twenty-five years ago the petty merchant, the *fellah* or the artisan from the Hebron area met his colleagues from Tiberias or Nazareth only very rarely . . . Nowadays, thanks to the new highways, motorized transport, market interests and working conditions and many other reasons, the separation between the various districts is overcome.'
>
> Last but not least, 'the slow ripening of the political programme of the Palestinian Arabs'. There is, according to Arlosoroff, a growing sophistication in the articulation of the political demands among the Arabs, and it is beginning to focus on the call for the constitution of a Palestinian national assembly: such a demand, founded as it is on democratic and parliamentary principles of self-determination and majority rule, would give the Arabs a majority role in deciding the future destiny of the country, based on universal-

istic principles which the Zionist movement would find very difficult to object to publicly.*

Yet for all of these developments of Arab nationalism in Palestine in the years between 1921–29, Arlosoroff argued that because of the non-confrontational policies of the Zionist movement, the Palestinian Arab movement was still divided among various groups and clans, and the radical element had been losing ground. The call for a Legislative Assembly did not excite the *fellah*, and because the general atmosphere in the country had been tranquil, Palestinian-Arab nationalism, while constantly growing, had not really hampered the Zionist enterprise.

With the attempts of the right-wing Revisionists to focus attention on the Wailing Wall, this uneasy equilibrium had been shattered, and a new, highly flammable and emotional issue had been thrust into the limelight:

> With protests against the Balfour Declaration one could not arouse a dog from his comfortable place beside the fireside. The demand for a parliament is for the *fellah* too abstract, and does not awaken his instincts. ... Even the immigration of 100,000 Jews and the purchase of 1,000,000 dunams of land would not have stirred the Muslims in Egypt and Bombay in the least ...[15]

Yet the Revisionist provocation around the Wailing Wall had ignited an element of religious fanaticism among Palestinian Arabs, which had swept through the wider

* Arlosoroff is alluding here to the idea, which constantly came up during the period of the British Mandate, to convene an elected Legislative Assembly in Palestine as a transitional step towards self-rule, as had been the case in the other Mandates in the Middle East (Syria, Iraq). Vesting power in the hands of such an assembly would deliver the *Yishuv* into the hands of the Arab majority in Palestine, and the idea was always viewed with suspicion by the Zionist movement, despite the obvious difficulties such an approach presented to Zionism as a movement committed to the idea of self-determination.

reaches of the Arab and Muslim world. It was the most dangerous and stupid thing from the Zionist perspective to get into a confrontation involving Muslim holy sites:

> How did we allow ourselves to be pushed into a hopeless policy of prestige; how did it happen that around us a system of provocations should develop, built up and directed with cunning; that we make out of an issue which has never been at the centre of our world [the Wailing Wall] a new idol; that we gave the Arab radicals a weapon which they can turn against us, not only with regard to the Palestinian *fellah*, but also with regard to the whole of the Muslim world; that we conduct a politics of bravura, which runs contrary to our main interests and which culminated in the bloody weeks we have experienced . . .
>
> Thus [the Arab extremists] were given an opportunity to inflate artificially a religious conflict, to manipulate the fanaticism and ignorance of the Arab masses and to mobilize for political purposes the dark forces of religious animosity.[16]

These developments had, according to Arlosoroff, given a great impetus to the dormant Arab movement, and made it possible for the Mufti and his people to spread their propaganda outside the borders of Palestine by making Jerusalem into a symbolic centre for the whole Arab and Muslim world; the radical clans among the Palestinians—the Husseinis—had been strengthened; Arab youth organizations had been fuelled with a powerful new symbolism—'Save the holy sites of Islam'; this also created an almost incongruous Islamic-Communist alliance.[17]

Again, what should the Zionist response be? First of all, Arlosoroff argues, Zionists should stop denying the reality of the situation and squarely face the existence of an Arab-Palestinian national movement: this does not detract, in any way, from the legitimacy of Zionism. The response should not result, on the other hand, in losing faith in the ability of the Zionist movement to realize its aims. It is for this reason, despite all his fiery criticism of Revisionist extremism, that Arlosoroff is equally critical of people like Judah Leib Magnes and the Brith Shalom movement who, under the impact of Arab hostility, were ready to give up altogether the hope of achieving Jewish independence in Eretz Israel. While condemning all premeditated provocations against Arab sentiments and Muslim sensibilities, the movement should, according to Arlosoroff, continue its programme of immigration and settlement, and constantly aim at increasing the Jewish population: any interruption in the constructive Zionist effort would only raise the level of hopes on the Arab side. Furthermore, the Zionist movement should establish institutions aiming to help Arab *fellahin* with credit and economic development and existing Jewish institutions already active in this field should be further expanded.[18]

Arlosoroff goes one step further, trying to find allies for the Zionist cause among Arabs outside Palestine: Zionism should not be construed, by either Jews or Arabs, as being opposed to Arab national aspirations as such, despite the existing conflict over Palestine:

> It may again mean the following: support for the demands of the Egyptians and the Syrians for progress and freedom, to be expressed throughout the world by the Jewish and Zionist press; perhaps it should also mean that we should send emissaries to Cairo and Baghdad in order to clarify that we have no interest in opposing the justified demands of the inhabitants of these countries—on the contrary, that we are ready to support them according to our abilities.[19]

This is a bold and unorthodox idea of a diplomatic offensive—and in a different guise Arlosoroff resorts to other novel ideas a few years later, knowing that it will mean a possible clash with the British government. He combined this idea with a suggestion 'to send a group of our students to Al-Azhar University' to study Muslim and Arab culture; this is not merely a tactical move, but suggests a readiness for an overall re-orientation of the Zionist approach to relations between the Zionist movement and Arab society at large, including the various Arab nationalist movements in the surrounding countries. There is no doubt that Arlosoroff's acquaintance, through his previous studies, with nationalism as a modern universal phenomenon made it easier for him than for other Zionist leaders and thinkers, who lacked a comparable background, to try to reach out to what he recognized as a cognate movement among the Arab societies surrounding Palestine.[20]

These plans for the future did not diminish Arlosoroff's awareness of the fact that if the extremism of the Revisionists was allowed to continue, it would pose a grave danger not only to conciliation with the Arabs, but to the very continuation of the Zionist enterprise. He viewed the Revisionists' programme as unrealistic and utterly dangerous: for example, Jabotinsky's plans for a Jewish armed force under British Imperial aegis hurt the chances for a realistic increase in Jewish recruitment to the Palestine Police. But the gravest danger arising from the Revisionist position was an educational one, as Jabotinsky's theories helped to create a myth and a cult of Jewish power without the realities of power:

> The decisive danger . . . is in the [Revisionist] movement's spiritual and psychological influence. Revisionist propaganda created, especially among certain younger circles, a nationalistic phraseology about rule by force, without having created—or being able to create—the means for such a rule . . . It is a tragedy that some conflicts cannot be solved except by force . . . But if one burdens a powerless people, lacking external

> means of power and fighting for its very survival, with a bloated programme of gestures and illusions, totally devoid of reality—then a terrible caricature is being created. A movement and a younger generation educated in this spirit are doomed to be broken and shattered with the destruction of these empty illusions and gestures.[21]

Again, as in the past, the 'constructivist' nature of Arlosoroff's socialist Zionism led him to a middle position between the militant chauvinism of the Revisionists and the despair of the pacifist Brith Shalom: the Zionist enterprise had to continue and would not be abandoned because of the use of force by the Arabs. On the other hand, Zionism should not look for confrontation, nor should it seek to provoke the Arab population: it should continue, despite the difficulties, and despite the anger at expressions of murderousness on the part of Arab nationalism, with the building of the new society in Eretz Israel. Arlosoroff admitted that this policy of trial and error might not be welcome 'from the point of view of abstract logic or aesthetics'.[22] It was, however, to him the only policy which was both morally defensible and realistically possible.

## III

For all Arlosoroff's criticism of the Revisionists' heavy responsibility for highlighting the tensions between Jews and Arabs in 1929, he realized that regardless of who was to blame and in what proportions, the conditions of Palestine had changed dramatically and had become more violent. Arlosoroff had always been aware that what the British Administration in Palestine really wanted was to support neither the Jews nor the Arabs: all they wanted was, basically, to maintain peace and quiet, and whoever appeared to rock the boat would be severely curtailed by them. He thus realized that one of the consequences of the 1929 disturbances would be even less British enthusiasm and support for implementing those policies of the Zionist Organization which would tend to further inflame Arab susceptibilities. One difficulty which he foresaw (and subsequent British policies proved him right) was that it would be increasingly difficult for Jews to be able to buy land in Palestine—and this he judged to be a most serious obstacle for the further development of Zionism and the *Yishuv*. This became an ever more burning issue in the early thirties, with the deteriorating situation of European Jewry.

Arlosoroff was looking for ways to lessen the danger of the worsening relations between Jews and Arabs if Jewish immigration were to increase significantly. In his quest he came up with a number of unconventional and unorthodox ideas; given his standing, since 1931, as Head of the Political Department of the Jewish Agency for Palestine, this gave his ideas a concrete turn, and they were indeed expressed in a number of speeches before closed sessions of various institutions within the Zionist movement and his own party.[23]

The first of these unorthodox ideas was to try to purchase land for Jewish settlement in Transjordan, and Arlosoroff was in touch with both Emir Abdullah of Transjordan (the grandfather of King Hussein of Jordan) as well as with some Transjordanian notables and sheikhs. The motivation for this step was not (as it has been with the Revisionists' claim for 'both banks of the Jordan') that Transjordan was part of the biblical Jewish homeland or even that, prior to 1922, it was included in the British Mandate for Palestine. Other Zionist leaders had made similar attempts, but Arlosoroff's was, on the contrary, a pragmatic (and, eventually, unsuccessful) attempt to lessen the tensions with the Arab population in Palestine itself. It certainly was a very circuitous way to achieve this, yet it reveals something about the creativity and political wisdom of Arlosoroff's thinking.

In two speeches, one to the Executive of the Jewish

Agency on 28 September, 1932, and the other to the Central Committee of the Mapai Labour Party on 19 January, 1933, Arlosoroff reported that economic conditions in Transjordan had pushed the Emir and some of the local notables to seek contact with leaders of the *Yishuv* in order to alleviate their economic plight by selling land to Jewish organizations. Arlosoroff suggested that the Zionist movement should carefully consider these proposals for a number of reasons.

First and foremost, Arlosoroff reminded his listeners that within the confines of Western Palestine, it had become increasingly more difficult to buy additional land for Jewish settlement due to the intensification of Arab nationalist propaganda in the wake of the 1929 disturbances. Moreover, even in cases where land could be purchased, the very fact of the purchase tended to exacerbate tensions and supply the extremists among the Arabs with ammunition for their anti-Zionist propaganda. In cases where Arab tenants, even if they were few and fully compensated, were being evicted from their holdings because of these purchases, such occurrences became major news not only in Palestine but also in England and created public difficulties for the Zionist movement in the British Parliament and the press. In other words, purchasing land in Western Palestine was either impossible or so fraught with political entanglement, public friction and negative publicity that it turned out to be an almost insurmountable obstacle.

In Transjordan, on the other hand, Arlosoroff argued, there were enormous tracts of totally unpopulated land. If some of these lands could pass into Jewish hands, no friction would occur with the local Arab population, and, because these areas were far away from the nationalist centres of Palestinian Arabs in Jerusalem and Jaffa, hardly any attention would be paid to such transactions in the Arab community itself. An increase of the Jewish population in Transjordan would not cause the kind of tension which any increase in Jewish settlement activities in Western Palestine would have caused. Such a policy would avoid confrontation while at the same time it would widen the basis of the Jewish population. Arlosoroff added that the purchase of land in Transjordan might also lead to creating friendly relations with the local leaders and chieftains in the area, who were not imbued with the kind of nationalism characterizing Palestinian Arabs proper.[24]

This is a highly complex and unorthodox argument, combining *raison d'état* with a non-confrontational approach. From the outset it might have been too convoluted to be politically feasible: as things turned out, nothing ever came of the idea, despite some very intensive contact between Arlosoroff and the political leaders of Transjordan. In any case, Arlosoroff was assassinated a few months after his second speech on this issue. But the episode shows the versatility and originality of Arlosoroff's thought in his attempt to minimize friction with the Arab population in Palestine.

More than fifty-five years later, the conflict between Jews and Arabs within the historical boundaries of Eretz Israel is still not over. Many of the arguments, both between Jews and Arabs, as well as within Israeli society in the 1980s, are surprisingly similar to those with which Arlosoroff had to contend. For his part, Arlosoroff was far from being a starry-eyed *naïf*, and he realized that some conflict might be unavoidable. He still basically believed that Jewish and Palestinian-Arab nationalism could co-exist if the political leadership on both sides was ready for a mutual compromise, and had the courage to lead their people in this direction.

# 5
# CONFRONTING THE BRITISH EMPIRE

## I

The complex relationship between the Zionist movement and Great Britain can be traced in the evolution of Arlosoroff's attitude towards the British Administration in Palestine and the British Empire in general. Like other Zionist leaders, Arlosoroff's attitude oscillated between viewing Britain as the mainstay of support for a Jewish National Home and a deep suspicion that Britain regarded Zionism—and its commitments to it as expressed in the Balfour Declaration and the League of Nations Mandate over Palestine—as a nuisance and an obstacle to its imperial interests which called for close co-operation with the Arabs in the Middle East. Like other socialist Zionists, Arlosoroff also felt the inherent ambiguity, if not outright contradiction, in trying to develop a Jewish socialist commonwealth under the wings of the British Empire. That this Empire was presided over, for some considerable period during that time, by a Labour Government in Westminster, with the Fabian theoretician Sidney Webb, elevated to the House of Lords as Lord Passfield, as Colonial Secretary, only added to this ambiguity.

Many of the leaders of the *Yishuv* in the 1920s were also inherently suspicious of the British Administration in Palestine on a personal level: for many of them, coming from the Eastern European Jewish Pale of Settlement, their dealings with British colonial officers were sometimes the first contact they may ever have had on a significant level with Gentiles; and the basic suspicion of many *shtetl* Jews towards the *goyim* never totally left them.

Arlosoroff was one of the few Palestinian Jewish leaders at the time—and perhaps the only one in the socialist Zionist leadership—who, through his immersion in Russian and German culture as well as in European university life, was relatively free from that ambivalence characterizing such *galuth* mentality, and able to face British officials on an equal footing without being aggressive about it.

The breadth of Arlosoroff's background and education reveals itself in a number of his writings, especially in an essay on *The British Administration and the Jewish National Home* (1928). It is one of the more perceptive studies of the nature of British adminstration in Palestine—and the mentality of British colonial officialdom in general. Here Arlosoroff attacks the ethno-centric and short-sighted view of those Zionists who attribute every disagreement on the part of the British officials with any Zionist claim or policy to anti-Semitism: 'How superficial this is one can judge from the fact that almost no member of the high echelons of the [British] Administration [in Palestine] has been excluded from such accusations.'[1] A much more sophisticated approach is necessary, and given Arlosoroff's penchant for sociological typology, he distinguishes three groups among the British officials in the country:

The first category, which according to Arlosoroff comprises perhaps 10% of the British Administration in Palestine, are people of high intelligence and broad education and culture: they are at home in the world of ideas, are themselves imbued with idealism, and many of them have come to Palestine with a fair knowledge of the Jewish problem. These people generally tend to be friendly to the

Zionist enterprise, 'though this still does not cause them to speak out and act as if they were members of the Zionist Actions Committee'.[2] In this category Arlosoroff names the two former Chief Secretaries of the Mandatory Government of Palestine, Sir Wyndham Deedes and Sir Gilbert Clayton.

The second group belongs in quality to the same background as the first in terms of ideas and learning, but they are not as well-versed in Jewish affairs; they are not hostile to the Jews, but they understand their burden of Empire as a responsibility towards the welfare of the 'natives'—i.e., the Arabs. In this category Arlosoroff mentions Gertrude Bell (a former close collaborator of Lawrence of Arabia) and St. John Philby, the advisor to Emir Abdullah.*

The bulk of the British officials (two-thirds according to Arlosoroff) includes 'most police officers and N.C.O.s, Post Office directors, the architects working for the Departments of Public Works, Health and the Land Registry'. They are basically practical people, and when they have to decide on such issues as whether to allow the usage of Hebrew in the Post Office or give permission for a procession to the Tomb of Simon the Righteous, their considerations are drawn from practicality and prudence, not from ideology or sympathy—or lack of it—towards Zionism. All that these minor British officials want is to keep order, have as few troubles as possible and not to rock the boat or get into the middle of a controversy which may make them appear incompetent as administrators. Of the ideological merits of the case they know little and care even less:

> When [these officials] come to Palestine, they hardly know anything about it, and before coming here they have probably never heard about Zionism. The worldwide Jewish question interests them as much as last

* Philby later converted to Islam. His son was Kim Philby, the Soviet mole in MI6.

> year's snow. They know nothing about our immigration and settlement intentions, and have no opinion in general about our enterprise. To my view, neither do they have any prejudices against us.[3]

Nevertheless Arlosoroff is aware of the fact that most of these basically neutral, indifferent and decent colonial administrators sooner or later tend to become more sympathetic to the Arab than the Jewish cause. Since Arlosoroff does not think that anti-Semitism can be an adequate answer in most cases, what are the reasons for this development?

Arlosoroff suggests a structural explanation for this tendency, which transcends individual behaviour and personal case histories; it is rooted in the basic fact that the Zionist enterprise does not fit into the general world-view and life experience of a British colonial administrator. Most of them come to Palestine from other colonies ('Just like their Roman predecessors eighteen centuries ago', Arlosoroff cannot refrain from remarking ironically) and they are used to a well-oiled administrative machine: those who disrupt their routine, or do not fit into its basic conceptual framework, are naturally viewed with suspicion. The Zionist demands and policies, because of their uniqueness and singularity, cannot easily fit into a handbook of colonial administration. Many of these officials also come to Palestine after having served in the Sudan, Egypt or Iraq, and feel comfortable with the Arabs, whose behaviour, seen by them as a combination of obsequiousness, innate courtesy and expected hypocrisy and duplicity, they know how to handle. The Jews, on the other hand, are a dilemma, maintains Arlosoroff, portraying with some empathy the bafflement of a British colonial officer confronted by pioneering *halutzim*: if faced by a group of primitive Arab labourers who are hired to construct a road, a British Public Works official knows what to expect—including the petty thievery involved. But, Arlosoroff makes him ponder

> ... if I take Jewish workers, I will have under my command people who learned their trade only a few years ago. Every one of them speaks five languages (by itself a rare phenomenon among people who are not Communist agitators). Some of them have formerly been students, and others were tailors and cobblers. They say they are here due to an Historical Process and because of it they have become construction workers. But what do I have to do with an Historical Process ...? Compared to the Arabs, every Jew, the whole *Yishuv*, appears an inorganic, mystical and unusual being ...
>
> What made these people leave their more or less developed countries and come to this poor and rocky Oriental land? What makes the son of an industrialist live in a hut and the daughter of a banker live in a log-cabin and eat three meals a day consisting of beans and olives? What is the link which is welding together the American middle-class Jew from Tel Aviv and the Yemenite porter, the graduate of a German university and the Russian member of *Hovevei Zion*, the Anglo-Jewish High Commissioner [Sir Herbert Samuel] and the merchant from Bokhara? To the British officials all this is strange and utterly abnormal.[4]

Added to this, continues Arlosoroff, many British officials are imbued with the mystique of the Orient, which they readily identify in Palestine with the Arabs (even if the 'urban Palestinian Arabs' relationship to the Saudis and the Wahabbis may be questionable'.) The Jew, on the other hand, is perceived as a European—albeit an unusual one—and British colonial officials do not know how to relate to such a rare bird. But they have been trained in how to deal with the 'natives'.[5]

Arlosoroff's sociological insights, enlivened by self-deprecating humour (a rare commodity among Zionist thinkers), does not by itself lead to policy recommendations: his aim was to draw attention to a dilemma and counter the self-righteousness of so many Jews, as well as to point out that the demand of 'firing all the anti-Semitic elements in the Administration' is ridiculous and politically stupid. In an interesting aside he mentions that were there to exist some sort of parliamentary institution in Palestine, the activities of these officials would come under some scrutiny. But since Arlosoroff knows that the idea of such a Legislative Assembly is viewed with suspicion by most of the Zionist movement, as it would perpetuate the minority status of the Jews in Palestine, this was no more than a pious wish: but Arlosoroff mentions it nevertheless, appearing to suggest that there is a political price for every policy adopted by the Zionist movement.

But despite its inconclusive nature, this analysis of the social and cultural background of the British bureaucracy in Palestine is of significant theoretical value: it also shows that even in the daily tug-of-war of political manoeuvring and tactics, Arlosoroff was able to maintain the distance of a scholar—a rare phenomenon in the intense ideological and emotional atmosphere of so much Zionist writing and rhetoric of that period (and of subsequent ones).

## II

A further and even more critical attempt to confront the realities of the British Administration in Palestine occurred a few months before Arlosoroff's death, at a debate at the Mapai Labour Party Council in January 1933. Arlosoroff's lengthy discourse elicited a very critical response from some of his colleagues, among them David Ben Gurion; these exchanges were not published until 1984, and were not known outside Mapai's inner circles for many years.[6]

Arlosoroff's discourse combines the immediate concerns *vis-à-vis* the British Administration in Palestine with some wider dimensions of social and political theory characteristic of his approach to most practical problems of political daily life. The speech was made at the height of the political crisis in Germany which would bring the Nazis into power a mere fortnight later. The sense of urgency—the feeling that some radical re-thinking was necessary in face of the new realities—can be gleaned from some of the truculence and impatience of Arlosoroff's formulations, as well as from his readiness to clash head-on with two of the most powerful leaders of Mapai—David Ben Gurion and Yitzhak Tabenkin.

In his speech Arlosoroff attacks one of the more revered aspects of the conventional wisdom of the socialist Zionist movement in Eretz Israel: its unwillingness to take part in the administrative structures of the British Mandatory Government of Palestine. While always calling on the British Administration to remain true to the principles of the Balfour Declaration, the socialist Zionist parties shied away from actively participating in the Administration itself, preferring to develop the various organs of self-government of the Jewish community (such as the Jewish Agency, the *Va'ad Leumi,** etc.) as well as the wide-spread network of Histadruth enterprises which included not only the kibbutz and moshav movements but also co-operative industries, marketing societies, loan associations, etc. A consequence of this policy was not only opposition to the creation of a Legislative Assembly in Palestine, but also an opposition to extending government taxation, governmental control of land usage and water resources—all coupled with a suspicion, in many cases justified but not always so, of the machinations of perfidious Albion.

Arlosoroff argues in his speech that the outcome of this Zionist attitude was that the actual Palestinian state apparatus

* The National Committee of the Representative Assembly of the Jewish Community in Palestine.

as it was slowly emerging under British Mandatory control was turning out to be a veritable British-Arab administration with the Jewish ingredient heavily under-represented out of the free choice—and suspicion—of the Jews themselves. Such a structure naturally did not favour the Jewish population—which then complained of dark stratagems against it. And so the vicious circle went on, to the detriment of the Jewish role in the effective administration of the country.

This to Arlosoroff had far-reaching consequences, as the ultimate structure of the government of Eretz Israel would be determined by the realities of existing administrative structures, including such prosaic questions as personnel, staffing, etc. An actual Jewish state could not develop in the future *ex nihilo*, but would be grounded in and grow out of the existing Palestinian state structure—which would continue to develop under the British Mandate.[7]

Arlosoroff accused his own movement—and the Zionist Organization in general—of not realizing what the changes in the reality of Palestine had been since it came under British rule in 1917. Under the Ottoman Empire, Palestine was a marginal province of a large and decrepit empire. By his time, Palestine was a distinct political entity, and it was absurd for the socialist Zionist movement not to realize the consequences of this:

> There does exist a government in Eretz Israel, and its impact and influence on the life of the country becomes greater every year and penetrates more and more areas of activity . . . This is primarily so in budgetary matters . . . Twelve years ago the Zionist Executive had an annual budget of £1,000,000, and the Mandatory Government had a budget of £1,000,000 . . . Today, the Government of Palestine has an annual budget of £2,250,000 (and £1,000,000 surplus) and we have about £250,000 for activities and a deficit of £500,000 . . .
>
> Moreover, the utilization of the budget poses new

> administrative problems every year and constantly moves into new areas . . .[8]

According to Arlosoroff, the *Yishuv* was, paradoxically, sometimes the victim of the success of its self-government: because so many areas of Jewish life had been successfully catered for by the Jewish and Zionist organs of self-government (education, health, economic development, municipal affairs) the expansion of the scope of activity of the Mandatory Administration had tended to address itself almost exclusively to the needs of the Arab sector, with its low level of self-generated public welfare. The Jews, in a way, opted out of the emerging and developing Palestinian state, from which they had become constantly more and more alienated.

Arlosoroff enumerates various areas of government activity from which the Jewish community voluntarily opted out and suggested rethinking the traditional Zionist policies in these areas:

AGRICULTURAL DEVELOPMENT: it is true that the initial government impetus to help the Arab *fellahin* came from the perception that Jewish purchase of land had created a landless rural Arab population in the country, and that this sector of the Arab population deserved to be helped by government action. Naturally, Arlosoroff conceded, the *Yishuv* shied away from such policies. However, the problems of how to modernize the Arab agricultural sector had reached such proportions that it was now in the interest of the *Yishuv* itself to see to it that Arab agriculture became stronger, otherwise a crisis among Arab peasants would lead to anti-Zionist agitation and eventually to government policies unsympathetic to the Jewish population and its needs. Arlosoroff argued that only a wide-ranging agrarian reform in the Arab village and the intensification of agricultural methods would enable the *fellah* both to find adequate livelihood and make sure that there would be 'enough of a surplus of land which we should be able to buy. Otherwise, within a very short time we shall not be able to buy any more land, and neither the Government of Palestine, nor world public opinion, will allow us to do so.'[9]

TAX STRUCTURE: the Zionist Organization had consistently opposed the introduction of a progressive income tax, arguing that given the social differences in the structures of the Jewish and Arab communities in Palestine, the burden of such a tax would fall disproportionately on the Jewish sector, while most of the expenditure would be on the Arab population—this at a time when existing indirect taxes (customs, excise, etc.) were already largely carried by the Jewish population. Arlosoroff pointed out that even if true, such an argument was superficial, and for a socialist party to oppose income tax was an absurd and untenable position. Even if the Jews, who made up 18% of the population of Palestine, paid up to 40% of existing taxes and customs payments, a socialist party could not overlook the question of 'what kind of Jew is paying these taxes'. Rather than oppose income tax without qualification, the *Yishuv*—and Mapai—had to respond to the government initiative about income tax by agreeing to it—but on the condition that the already existing indirect taxes should be correspondingly adjusted so that the present disproportionately heavy burden of taxation on the Jewish community would not be worsened.

GOVERNMENT WATER POLICIES: the Government's proposal to control water resources was again considered by the Zionist movement as aimed at limiting Jewish access to water, thus curtailing further Jewish agricultural development. But Palestine *had* a water problem, and there was no way of denying this. Rather than automatically boycott every government attempt to regulate water resources, Jews should join the Water Boards proposed by the Administration, and *from within* try to ensure Jewish interests. Obstructionism was not an alternative to a policy, and to Arlosoroff was unacceptable.[10]

Arlosoroff gave further examples dealing with such issues as governmental support for private investment in municipal sewage works and water supply, governmental control of education and so on: in all these issues Arlosoroff strongly criticized his own party's equivocations and judged its policies to be questionable. He called for more Jewish participation in such government bodies as boards of education, water supply and land development, and argued that the way to ensure Jewish interest and influence was via participation, not ostracism and obstruction. He goes one step further to argue that more Jews should join the Administration as officials, adding

> I am not ashamed to say that in this field we have not done anything and have not even thought about it: not at the beginning, when the [British] Administration was established, and not now. Even today, when the government wants (rarely as it happens) to have new civil servants, when we can send people into the Administration, this is not being done . . . Even if it does not look as though we have many opportunities in this field, the scope of activities of the government is constantly expanding and we have slowly to take steps to extend our presence within the Administration.[11]

The reaction to Arlosoroff's ideas within his own party was one of fury. The speech was not only a challenge to much of socialist Zionist conventional wisdom, but coming from Arlosoroff, it was even more incongruous. After all, he belonged to the former Hapoel Hatzair wing of the unified Mapai Labour Party, and it was this wing, inspired by A. D. Gordon's Tolstoyan ideas, that always expressed a strong voluntaristic, ethical approach to social and political problems—as against the more power-oriented Poalei Zion people, who like Ben Gurion were occasionally accused of Bolshevik methods and mentality. And here was Arlosoroff, the 'ethical' socialist Zionist, calling for more participation in the state apparatus—and one controlled by the British imperial administration at that! Indeed, in the debate that followed, David Ben Gurion—since the early 1920s the Secretary-General of the Histadruth, who built its power as the most formidable social institution in the *Yishuv*—now lashed out at Arlosoroff for espousing 'etatist' ideas—a truly damning accusation within the labour movement, with particularly sinister undertones in the year 1933.

Arlosoroff's response to these accusations was a spirited one, in which he was able to make good use of his historical knowledge and intellectual acumen. Here the student of Sombart and the author of numerous studies on social and political movements and ideas brought his knowledge to bear on issues about which his colleagues, mostly self-educated Eastern European *heder* drop-outs from the *shtetl*, could only muster some half-baked and repetitive slogans. Having studied the thoughts of Pyotr Kropotkin in some detail, Arlosoroff felt that he understood such concepts as 'etatism' and 'autonomism' slightly better than Ben Gurion and Tabenkin;[12] and having been working at the time on an extensive study on *The History of Colonization* he also felt that his thoughts on how state power was created in societies based on overseas immigration and settlement were well founded.[13]

So when he responded, he was sufficiently well equipped not to be taken aback by the epitaph 'etatist' thrown at him. He gently chided his opponents not to get too entangled in abstract discussion about 'autonomism' and 'etatism', implying that perhaps they were not really up to the intellectual rigours of such a debate. But intellectual hauteur, bordering on arrogance, is hardly a useful weapon in the councils of a political party—and a labour party at that. So after a few jibes at the possible intellectual limitations of his opponents (who also happened to be the most prominent members of his own party), Arlosoroff returned to the historical observations he made in the body of his speech about the concrete conditions in Palestine and warned his party colleagues not to deny developments that were occurring before their own eyes because of ideological blinkers:

> What I wanted to explain was that the existing state in Palestine is increasing in power and is moving into new areas—yesterday it moved into land problems, today into the water question and tomorrow into what I don't even want to mention . . . I will not say whether this is desirable or undesirable. That is not my interest—the fact of the matter is, that it is happening. And I wanted to ask whether there can be a bridge between this development and our basic interests . . .
>
> If we have no answer to this challenge, developments will work against us . . .
>
> What we have experienced is that instead of a Jewish state we see that the state is developing separately—and the Jews are developing separately: and this is the danger which is threatening us and which we have to prevent.[14]

After somewhat coyly remarking that he did not really think that the debate between him and his opponents was one between autonomism and 'etatism', he added that in any case these two terms were not mutually exclusive: they were more analogous to the relations between the North Pole and the South Pole. He then came out with what was his strongest argument:

> But even if the two concepts complement each other, one cannot avoid the fact that in reality the theory of

> national autonomy is a theory of perpetual minorities, resigned to their eternal status as minorities. This is a natural theory for a people that cannot dream of becoming a nation state—like, for example, the Poles in Germany or the Germans in Czechoslovakia, who only want to guarantee their communal interests. For such a minority, the theory of autonomy is perfectly sufficient. But we have never resigned ourselves to such a theory with regard to Eretz Israel. We wanted to make the autonomous entity in the Land of Israel simultaneously into a territorial one, because we understood that autonomy in Eretz Israel has to be distinct from autonomy in the Diaspora and has to be founded on territorial rule . . .
>
> If we go beyond the right measure of autonomy, we will end up in total isolation and separation. And if this happens, not only our rights will suffer, but the growing and increasing state-power in the land will become an Arab power . . .[15]

Too much Jewish self-government, especially if it succeeds, may lead, according to Arlosoroff, to a dangerous isolationism; and the Jewish reluctance to partake of the governance of the land, may ultimately deliver the country into the hands of an Arab administration bolstered up by British policies. Many in the Zionist movement, setting their eyes on the ultimate aims of Zionism (the *Endziel* in the Zionist, as well as the socialist, jargon) had overlooked the dialectical links between reality as it was developing and its end product. Like Eduard Bernstein within the social democratic movement—but with different political aims in mind—Arlosoroff realized that Zionism had to deal with real, historical processes as they occurred, and not only with ultimate ends. If one remained outside the process, the ultimate destination might remain outside one's reach.

## III

These problems of understanding the processes of political power as it developed and evolved under the conditions of the British Mandate in Palestine are also at the core of an unusual and remarkable letter addressed by Arlosoroff to Dr Chaim Weizmann on 30 June, 1932.[16] It is an extremely long letter (nine closely typed pages), really an essay more than a letter; it is written in obvious anguish, weighing up the different options seen by Arlosoroff as open to the Zionist movement—and ending with the suggestion that it may be that the *Yishuv* would have no choice but to impose, under certain conditions, a dictatorship of the Jewish minority in Palestine in order to prevent a total collapse of the Zionist enterprise.

This extreme and radical position (never mentioned by Arlosoroff on any other occasion, whether in print or in a speech, nor ever presented by him in any way whatsoever to the Zionist Organization or to his own party) caused much public debate in the Zionist movement when the letter became public for the first time in 1949. It has occasionally been used by the Revisionist movement to suggest that towards the end of his life, Arlosoroff was moving in their direction—an interpretation naturally fiercely opposed by the followers of Arlosoroff within his own Labour movement.[17]

A careful analysis of Arlosoroff's letter suggests a much more complex picture. Radical as one of the four options raised by him undoubtedly is, the letter does not explicitly espouse it, nor does Arlosoroff suggest what steps should be taken to implement such a policy. There is no doubt that the letter is aimed to shock Weizmann, and this may perhaps explain why it was addressed to him—the most moderate among the Zionist leaders, then temporarily out of office in the Zionist Organization—rather than to someone like Ben Gurion, whose more activist approach might have been more attuned to such ideas. Neither does there exist a response by Weizmann to what must have been to him a very surprising line of argument.

In his characteristically forthright fashion, Arlosoroff raises in this letter—as he was to do several months later, albeit from a different angle to his January 1933 speech at the Mapai Council—a very fundamental question: with the scene of world politics changing so rapidly, can the aims of the Zionist movement be achieved within the existing and conventional structures of prevailing policies, or must some radical new thinking be done? Arlosoroff argues that the Zionist movement had reached the point where

> The Arabs are no longer strong enough to be able to destroy our position, yet . . . they believe themselves to be still powerful enough to enforce the establishment of an Arab state in Palestine without having regard to our political claims, while the Jews are sufficiently strong to be able to hold their ground, but not powerful enough to enforce the continuous growth of the *Yishuv* by immigration and settlement and to safeguard peace and order in the country during the process.

This is, to Arlosoroff, a considerable achievement if viewed from an historical perspective; but it suggests an equilibrium that may lead to stagnation and the eventual gradual disappearance of Zionism. A Zionist breakthrough would be guaranteed only if a new stage were achieved, 'when the balance of actual power will exclude any possibility of the establishment of an Arab state in Palestine'. Conventional Zionist thinking held that this could be achieved within the framework of the British Mandate. Arlosoroff then said bluntly, 'I tend to believe that it cannot.'

According to Arlosoroff, the 'evolutionary' Zionist policies, hitherto followed by the Zionist movement, had exhausted themselves: the qualitative jump now necessary could not be achieved through existing measures. The British Administration was at best lethargic and unmotivated, at worst not very friendly; Zionist means were limited; immigration levels were low; and no significant land reserves in Palestine were available.[18]

Under these conditions, with the likelihood of the Mandates in Syria and Iraq being terminated, leading to the establishment of Arab independent states in these areas, Arlosoroff saw in the next few years a strong pressure for the termination of the British Mandate and a similar move towards independence in Palestine—*with the Jews still in a minority*. This, according to Arlosoroff, was a distinct possibility, and the Zionist movement had better be prepared for such an eventuality. Equally worrying to Arlosoroff was the danger of a new world war, the outbreak of which he was certain, though he utterly mistook its circumstances and protagonists. The letter, after all, was written before the Nazis came to power in Germany:

> These developments could come to a sudden climax if, on top of all that, a new international armed conflict broke out in which the British Empire was involved. Can there be a doubt in anybody's mind that we are heading for a new great war? You may give it five years or ten. We may not know in what definite setting it will break out, whether it will come as a concentration against Soviet Russia (partly to prevent Bolshevism from spreading) or in another constellation. 'History,' to use Bismarck's phrase, 'does not allow us to look into her cards.' But where we are going can no longer be doubted.

In the face of such a grim prognosis, Arlosoroff sees four options before the Zionist movement:

> i. To muddle through, hoping that somehow things

will work out; this to Arlosoroff is the traditional *galuth* mentality of 'Jewish fatalism'. This cannot be a Zionist policy, as in this sense Zionism has always been, to Arlosoroff, 'a rebellion against Jewish tradition'.
ii. To admit that Zionism has been a failure and that it has no chance of achieving its aim: Arlosoroff did indeed discern such views among some of the followers of Magnes' Brith Shalom movement, as well as among those extreme left-wing socialist Zionists who became Communists, with some of them also returning to the Soviet Union, out of despair over Zionism.
iii. The partition of Palestine and the attempt to achieve a Jewish state in a part of the land.
iv. The establishment of a revolutionary Jewish dictatorship, aimed against both the British and the Arabs.

For obvious reasons Arlosoroff dismisses the first two options. His reservations about the third option—partition—are highly interesting, and eventually may help us to throw some light upon the whole underlying meaning of the letter to Weizmann. On the one hand, Arlosoroff admits that 'there is a sound core' to all the various schemes about partition, as they 'contain the elements of territorialism and political self-determination which are the fundamental truths of Zionism'. Yet, on the other hand, Arlosoroff feels that there are a number of insurmountable obstacles to partition, and he spells them out:

a. The limited size of Palestine.
b. The problems of Jerusalem.
c. The unfortunate geographical configuration of the areas of Jewish settlement (Coastal Belt, Emek,* Jordan Valley, Upper Galilee).

* the Jezreel Valley

> d. The fact that even in the above-defined districts the Jews form no more than a minority so that the problem is altered only quantitatively and not qualitatively.

The most crucial argument is, of course, the last: even under partition the demographic conditions of 1932 would not result in a Jewish majority even in that part of the Land of Israel that would be allotted to the Jewish State. The opposition to partition is for pragmatic, not ideological, reasons.

Since Arlosoroff declares that 'I should never accept the defeat of Zionism before an attempt was made which would be equal to the grim seriousness of our struggle for national life', he is ready to contemplate the fourth option, viz.:

> That Zionism cannot, in the given circumstances, be turned into a reality without a transitional period of the organized revolutionary rule of the Jewish minority, that there is no way for a Jewish majority, or even for an equilibrium between the two races (or else a settlement sufficient to provide a basis for a cultural centre) . . . without a period of a nationalist minority government which would usurp the state machinery, the administration and the military power in order to forestall the danger of our being swamped by numbers and endangered by a rising. During this period of transition a systematic policy of development, immigration and settlement would be carried out.

Arlosoroff is aware that such an approach 'may run counter to many beliefs which we have been holding for many years. It may come dangerously near certain popular political creeds with which we never had much sympathy.' Yet he is adamant that the Jewish people, in its hour of agony, may not totally rule out such an option. He also insists on trying to assuage Weizmann's alarm that this option should not be confused with Revisionist positions, which he views as irrational and unrealistic, especially in their reliance on the British 'to snatch the chestnuts out of the fire for us in keeping the Arabs down with their bayonets'. He continues to oppose the Revisionist views 'with their wholesale provocation which is not backed by any real power, producing militant reactions on the Arab side, stirring up and (indirectly) organizing forces which on the day of crisis will confront us'. Neither is Arlosoroff less critical of what he sees as the Revisionists' geo-political fantasies, 'engaged in vague searchings for a strategic basis between Paris, Warsaw and Rome'. He concludes, aware of how shocked Weizmann would be to receive such a letter, with expressing the hope that the latter would not think that 'I am getting out of my senses either'.

What is one to make of this? Is it an expression of despair, an emotional outburst written in a moment of low spirits during one of the nadirs of Zionist activity, caused—among other things—by the world-wide economic crisis? That Arlosoroff never proposed anything on these lines on any other occasion, nor tried this line of argument on any member or leader of his own party, clearly suggests that the 'fourth option' cannot be construed as a clear-cut policy choice: the whole letter is more in the nature of a 'position paper', trying out various alternatives—and throwing the most radical one into Weizmann's lap as shock treatment.

Perhaps the key to the processes of Arlosoroff's thought can be better understood by looking more carefully at his reservations about the option of partition. The major argument, we have seen, is demographic—i.e., that in the circumstances of 1932, even in the areas of dense Jewish settlement, the Jews were still only a minority. It is precisely this argument against partition which suggests that the letter to Weizmann was written in response to immediate considerations due to specific conditions, and that with a change in these, his views about partition might also change. It is idle to speculate what would have been Arlosoroff's view about partition when this became a real option—in other words, had he been alive when the Peel Commission Report came out or after World War II. But it is the realistic structure of his thought, which opposed partition not out of principle, but on the basis of the demographic data of 1932, which tends to suggest that with the change in the demographic structures of the country in the wake of the massive immigration of 1933-37 (which almost doubled the population of the *Yishuv*), Arlosoroff would not have seen the last option—that of the 'revolutionary dictatorship'—as the only feasible one any more. The partition option would by then have gained a completely new dimension and meaning—and it is a fact that less than half a year after the letter to Weizmann, in his Mapai speech of January 1933, Arlosoroff adopted a completely different tone about the relationship towards Britain: instead of a militant confrontation, he called for a utilization of the structure of the existing British Administration in Palestine to gain more influence and more power.

What is clear is that Arlosoroff—in his letter to Weizmann, in his 'etatist' speech to his colleagues in Mapai, in his attempts to try and purchase land in Transjordan in order to minimize friction with Palestinian Arabs—was looking for new policy alternatives. In this context, in his letter to Weizmann—his favourite Zionist senior statesman—he appears to be trying to play devil's advocate, bringing things to the limits of the possible, to suggest to Weizmann—and perhaps through him also to his British interlocutors—to what extreme positions British policies of the time might push even moderate, 'constructivist' Zionists like himself.

Anyone who sees in the 'fourth option' a concrete plan for action has, however, according to Arlosoroff, to ask himself a further question: what is the actual power base for such a dictatorship of the Jewish minority over the Arab majority, when the Arab majority will, presumably, be supported by the British, and the *Yishuv* will have *to fight both the British and the Arabs*? To a person like Arlosoroff, for whom realistic questions about the actual basis of power had always been at the centre of his thought and social analysis, this was a cardinal question: after all, Arlosoroff continually ridiculed the Revisionists for the unrealistic assumption of *their* policies.

It is, nevertheless, true that on the eve of the War of Independence in 1947-48 a situation arose that had some similarities to the scenario suggested by Arlosoroff in his fourth option. But there were three crucial differences: the *Yishuv* at that time was fighting against a much weakened British Empire, shorn of its power by World War II; moreover, the *Yishuv* itself was more than three times larger in 1947 than it had been in 1932, with not insignificant military experience gained during World War II. And, last but not least, the War of Independence was fought from the Zionist perspective on the basis of *the acceptance of partition*—and this was a very different situation from the one in the letter to Weizmann where the fourth option was premised on the dismissal of the partition option because of the demographic data of 1932.

Be this as it may, Arlosoroff's thinking about Britain and its relationship to Zionism and the *Yishuv* shows both the complexity and innovative nature of his mind. His sociological understanding of administrative structures and his dialectical analysis of the growth of political power through the processes in which it is wielded, made it possible for him to go beyond the various slogans then accepted in the Zionist movement and to try to understand how the relationship to Britain must be dynamic, as the historical situation itself was rapidly changing, both regionally and globally.

# 6
# FUTURE SOCIETY: A FEDERATION OF FREE COMMUNIST ASSOCIATIONS

## I

In his essay *Jewish People's Socialism*, Arlosoroff outlined the relevance of a socialist perspective for the Jewish national movement. We have seen how his socialist Zionist programme is grounded in a wider understanding of the achievements and dilemmas of the European socialist movement. In looking for Arlosoroff's vision of future society, we shall similarly encounter a synthesis of his general understanding of socialism and its application to the Jewish context. For the purpose of this juxtaposition we shall discuss only two of his writings—a lengthy essay on the Russian anarchist Pyotr Kropotkin published in 1921, and an article, based on a speech, delivered to the 1926 Hapoel Hatzair conference, entitled 'Class Warfare in the Conditions of Eretz Israel'. From both, the nature of Arlosoroff's voluntaristic, non-etatist socialism emerges—a unique, non-doctrinaire blend of anarchist ideas and social-democratic practices, consciously presented as an alternative to a Marxist orthodoxy based on rigid class polarization. The essay on Kropotkin clearly indicates that because of his ethical approach to socialism, the indebtedness of Arlosoroff to anarchist modes of thought became very pronounced.

In discussing Kropotkin's thought, Arlosoroff at the outset admits that it cannot be compared to the over-arching architectonic structure of Marxism, precisely because it is less 'rabbinical' and therefore does not 'pretend to determine a necessary truth for all and sundry'.[1] In this, however, Arlosoroff sees one of its main virtues.

The essay on Kropotkin—perhaps one of the best written in any language from within the socialist movement—starts by making a clear distinction between two kinds of anarchist thought: 'individual anarchism' is clearly distinguished by Arlosoroff from 'social anarchism': the first can be traced back to Max Stirner, the second to Fourier and Bakunin.[2] Both trends have not, despite their doctrine, become mass movements, and are best studied by the scrutiny of the writings of individuals, not through an historical survey of political movements.[3]

The two schools of anarchist thought are, according to Arlosoroff, deeply divided in their relationship and attitudes to the social realm as such. 'Individualistic anarchism', he argues, is a legitimate heir to bourgeois liberalism, taking individualism to the extreme; as such it is not interested in social structures and social reforms, and should not really be linked at all with socialist thought. 'Social anarchism', on the other hand, is a variety of socialist thought and has much more in common with socialism than with the first brand of anarchism. It is the second brand of anarchism which interests Arlosoroff, and it is in this context that his study of Kropotkin is being presented.

In discussing the origins of Kropotkin's thought, Arlosoroff points out how much his method of scientific enquiry owes to the positivism of Comte and Spencer. But this should not draw attention away from the fact that Kropotkin's major inspiration came from Rousseau and his quest for a community. The positivistic methodology should not, according to Arlosoroff, make us lose sight of the communitarian drive in Kropotkin's thought.

This determines the premises of Kropotkin's critique of contemporary society. If Stirner and his brand of 'individualistic anarchists' start from the ego and individual self-interest and self-gratification, Kropotkin sees in solidarity 'the strongest and most constant cause of historical progress'. As against a social Darwinism of the war of all against all (individuals, groups, classes and species) Kropotkin posits the elements of association and co-operation for mutual help as the main spring of human action.[4]

Arlosoroff points out that this view of human co-operation is opposed to both bourgeois liberalism *and* Marxism: both liberals and Marxists see self-interest as the central motivation of activity. Arlosoroff reiterates Kropotkin's references to Marx's own admission that his views on class struggle have followed in the steps of theories developed by bourgeois thinkers, especially Guizot.[5] Kropotkin for his part maintains that while not all periods of human history have witnessed competition, egotism and the war of all against all, 'there is not one period, there is not one form of society ... in which we do not find solidarity and mutual help'. As an example of this Kropotkin gives the Middle Ages, and Arlosoroff joins him in retrieving the communitarian tradition of medieval Europe from later simplistic bourgeois views:

> The Middle Ages appear as a surprising, new, enchanting and creative period ... The nineteenth century, nurtured on rationalism and superficial materialism, sees the Middle Ages, from beginning to end, as a period of darkness and barbarism, of servility and ignorance, and this stereotype it bequeathed to the education of future generations.
>
> Kropotkin, on his part, tries at least to shed some light on the other side of this period: on medieval

> communal life, on the Communes of the Italian Renaissance and the burgher republics of Germany, within whose walls there flowed, to an extraordinary extent, liberty, social equality and all forms of mutual help. Kropotkin also retrieved the memory of this society which still possessed living, immediate social relationships; he reminds us of the social organism of the guilds, the Common Law and personal liberty; and of the living tradition and its forms deeply ingrained in the masses of the toiling people.[6]

While Arlosoroff may have been carried away by this romantic reconstruction of medieval life—common not only to Kropotkin but also to the German intellectual ambience within which Arlosoroff himself had been educated—he goes on to quote Kropotkin's contention that even in modern capitalist society 'there exist kernels of future Communist society—from the Communist element of street lighting, water supply, etc., to the even stronger co-operative movement and all forms of proletarian unity'.[7]

It is the connection between private property and the state which Kropotkin sees, according to Arlosoroff, as the basis of social oppression: and while his premises clearly derive from Rousseau, the social criticism of the role of the state is close to that of Marx. Private property is to Kropotkin the quintessential expression of egotism and self-seeking, and the state emerges historically as the expression of this attempt to guarantee, institutionally and morally, the continuous control of the property owners not only over their property, but also over the property-less. The emergence of the state as a class-founded mechanism of domination and control started, according to Kropotkin, in the Middle Ages with the gradual disappearance of the village common and its appropriation by robber barons, eventually leading to the transformation of free peasants into serfs. To safeguard this appropriation, there emerged the power of the late medieval and early modern state as the enemy of freedom:

> Hundreds of years have passed, and in this period the rule of force has constantly changed form, but its essence remained and is the same: it strangles liberty, robs the will, is responsible for social oppression and supports private property and egoistic interests. And finally there is born, at the apex of development, the ultimate expression of class rule and the mainstay of social oppression: the contemporary centralized state.[8]

We have seen that Arlosoroff does not subscribe to a simplistic view of class: but it is the libertarian—though socially-oriented—element in Kropotkin's thought which he finds so enticing: Kropotkin's anarchism is rooted in his understanding of state power *per se* as being an instrument of oppression and class control, and hence he maintains that no proletarian emancipation from capitalism is possible so long as the state—in *any* form—continues to exist. Moreover—and it is here that Kropotkin so strongly diverges from Marx—trying to substitute a socialist state (even in a period of transition) for the existing capitalist one will not emancipate the worker; it will merely mean exchanging one form of control for another. Kropotkin is aware of the dangers of the emergence of a New Class within socialist society, and it is here that Arlosoroff turns Kropotkin's warning against 'socialist etatism' into a resounding critique of the Bolshevik experiment:

> The monopoly of power has to disappear. Hence [Kropotkin] perceives in his sharp vision the new danger standing between freedom and the working man. Many years before the victory of Bolshevism . . . this Russian anarchist discovered the internal lie in any form of a proletarian state and declared his everlasting

> enmity to all those apparent revolutionaries, who strive to turn the redemptive labours of socialism into a kind of a grand new state capitalism. Among the ruins of the capitalist state he discovers the emergence of a new slavery. A New Class begins to emerge, trying to concentrate in its hands the power held by the old state.
>
> In place of the White Army comes the Red Army, in place of the White bureaucrat—the Red bureaucrat, in place of White Power—Red Power, and the victim of the New State will once more be the people, whose name is taken in vain by all those battalions of Commissars.
>
> Kropotkin is as hard as rock about this one conviction: socialism will have to be a socialism of freedom, an anti-etatist socialism, an anarchist socialism—or the socialist idea will never succeed.[9]

This libertarian socialist view is also at the root of Arlosoroff's own vision of future society in general—and in Palestine in particular. His vision of the kibbutz in the socialist Zionist context is seen within a wider horizon of a communitarian, voluntaristic society, where state power is supplanted by the free association of human groups. This view of a world of communes, freely associated with each other, is as much Arlosoroff's expression of his global as well as of his immediate, Zionist future society:

> One commune will join another, or a group of communes, only if it sees it as necessary for its own existence. In such a free league of communes, the communes will regulate their joint affairs through co-operation. Out of this a harmonious associated future society will emerge ... the nation as a great federation of free, communist associations.[10]

Arlosoroff insists that this is not a Utopian pipe dream: according to him, Kropotkin has discerned the processes which within capitalist society itself—unbeknownst to capitalist ideologues as well as to Marxist critiques—are basically transforming it from competitive to co-operative modes of behaviour. These processes are: the introduction of self-management in many enterprises; the further development—contrary to predictions about centralization—of small-scale manufacture in Russia, France, Germany and even England; the intensification of agriculture, etc. Yet Arlosoroff warns that these developments are not happening automatically, and he sees Kropotkin falling into the same cognitive trap of quasi-determinism as the Marxists.[11] Yet despite this critique of Kropotkin's progressivist, linear vision of history, Arlosoroff still sees his vision as the most noble one within the socialist and anarchist tradition—mainly because it is not in thrall to 'the hypnosis of power':

> This is the new and free society of universal welfare; a society without government, a society of communist anarchism. This vision of a world to come Kropotkin provides not in exalted hymns and psalms, but in the most popular of words and most simple of images. Society is not founded on power, neither is it a dictatorship of a minority or a majority, nor is it seen as an external necessity, whether appearing as a title to property or a policeman's baton, whether it is a military command or a government regulation. The basis of society is founded on free will, on an association without government, on the *élan vital* which anarchist terminology calls *Libre Entente*.
>
> Our generation's thought has been so much confined by the vicious circle of the idea of power that we cannot picture to ourselves this free association . . .[12]

Writing in 1921, with the Bolshevik experience, which split the socialist movement, before his eyes, Arlosoroff sees in Kropotkin's vision an alternative to Leninist tyranny, as well as to the uninspiring bureaucratization of the social-democratic movement in the West. He wistfully concludes his essay with these remarks, bringing out the literary and imaginative qualities of his writing:

> But when the decisive period in the history of mankind arrives and the war of freedom breaks out among the nations, Kropotkin's courageous words are destined to enrich, whether consciously or not, the thinking of those fighters and provide a new impetus for moral thought.
>
> And during that battle, when the defenders of the *status quo*—and in those days such a role will perhaps be in the hands of the Soviet of the Proletarian State or the Chief of the Proletarian Police—try to stifle this core of immortal freedom with bans, prisons, states of emergency and press censorship—then the revolutionaries of the day-after-tomorrow will be able to draw from the treasure of Kropotkin's ideas power, advice, motivation, will and the holy spirit of life.[13]

It is these universal concerns of the democratic socialist movement—confronting both capitalism as well as the Bolshevik experience in Russia—which are at the heart of Arlosoroff's choosing Kropotkin's social anarchism as a model for his own vision of future society. Immersed as Arlosoroff was in developing his vision of a socialist Zionism, the universal dimensions of the socialist movement were never lost to him.

## II

Finding in Kropotkin an ally for his version of a voluntaristic form of socialism, inspires Arlosoroff also in his quest for articulating the structures of a Jewish socialist society in Palestine. Such a libertarian socialism, tinged with anarchism and motivated by ethical considerations, is at the core of his programmatic speech to the 1926 conference of Hapoel Hatzair in Palestine. This speech is as much a polemic against the attempts by Zionist Marxists to transfer to Eretz Israel the materialistic class concepts of Marxism, as his essay on Kropotkin was similarly an attempt to present an alternative to a rigid class-ridden view of socialism. The speech follows the main arguments of his *Jewish People's Socialism*—but while in that essay the perspective is still that of a socialist Zionist in the Diaspora, the 1926 speech is already deeply immersed in the Palestinian experience and in what can be learned from it for the future of a socialist society in Eretz Israel.[14] In analyzing this speech one should constantly bear in mind that Hapoel Hatzair, for all its commitment to being a 'workers' party' and its insistence on the centrality of labour, had some unease with using the word 'socialist' because of its identification with Marxism (and with the Marxist Zionist Poalei Zion—its main rival on the Zionist left). Arlosoroff, on the other hand, had no such reluctance and was well equipped to distinguish his own brand of socialism from that of the Marxian tradition.

Arlosoroff argues that within the international socialist movement, when speaking of class power, socialists had a number of aims in mind: wresting political power from the hands of the bourgeoisie; achieving recognition for the workers' part in national culture; redistributing wealth and extending workers' control into various forms of industry. According to Arlosoroff, all of these targets are irrelevant in Palestinian reality, since a capitalist society does not exist there. On the other hand, national culture in Eretz Israel is virtually borne by the workers movement—so again the European paradigm of breaking into cultural life does not apply:

> As for the public standing of the worker and his integration into the cultural and artistic treasures—in

> this field, there is no basis for class warfare in the *Yishuv*. Since the workers' movement has been from its very inception—together with the teachers and the writers who joined it—the carrier of the nations' cultural renewal, of the renaissance of the language, and has held a pioneering role in cultural activities generally, it can be said that overall cultural life in the country has been founded by the workers' movement ... The public standing of the worker in our culture is without parallel: the organized labour movement in Eretz Israel is not a movement of 'the proletariat'. The Histadruth is the 'aristocracy' ... The organized worker is the hegemonic group in society—in the first Representative Assembly [of Palestinian Jews], 48% of the delegates were workers ...[15]

Because the economic structure of Jewish Palestine had still to be developed, the worker was involved in the basic endeavour of *creating* wealth, not dealing with its redistribution. It is also for this reason that there could be no defined and differentiated classes in the Jewish community in Palestine: if there was no capitalism, obviously there could not be a proletariat on the European model. Yet Arlosoroff pointed to the paradox that while there was no differentiated proletariat, there existed a working class *consciousness* in Palestine, and on this occasion he made a sophisticated use of a central Marxian concept about class:

> Having checked all these areas, we have to confront the fact that the theory of class war does however exist [in Palestine] as a mere 'fact of consciousness' in the psychology of thousands of workers. There exists a deep gap between the reality which we have studied and the consciousness living in broad sectors of the workers in Eretz Israel. Such gaps between reality and consciousness have existed also in other countries, but

> there it always appears to be the other way round. Marx in his *Eighteenth of Brumaire* points out that the petty peasantry of France—the majority of the population at the time of Napoleon III—were, objectively speaking, an economically developed class, but did not possess a consciousness about this. They were a class 'by itself', but not 'for itself'. In our case it is precisely the opposite. The workers of Eretz Israel are a class in their own eyes, 'for themselves', before they have become a class 'by themselves'. Such a gap between reality and consciousness would have been impossible if our ideology had developed only out of the conditions of Eretz Israel: it became possible only due to the importation of ideas.[16]

It was because of this difference between objective social and economic conditions in Palestine as compared to the industrialized West that socialism in Palestine could not be developed according to theories that have no relationship to local realities. Yet the *aims* of socialist Zionists have to be understood in the general context of the socialist movement, and the discrepancy in the objective conditions should not lead to the discarding of these aims and the vision inherent in them—i.e. the public control of national assets. This, like any other aspect of socialist theories, has to be adapted to local conditions, the primary one of which will be that 'Eretz Israel be mainly a country of labouring agriculture and not of centralized industry . . . Consequently the modes of socialist realization here will be much closer to those of Denmark than to those of England and Germany.'[17]

The reference to Denmark has an ironic twist: most socialist Zionists, nurtured as they were on the debates among Russian and German socialists which constantly referred to conditions in those countries while comparing them to England and France, have habitually tended to compare the humble conditions of Palestine—with less than

200,000 Jews—to conditions in those major European powers. Arlosoroff, by drawing attention to Denmark, also suggests to his colleagues to be less fixated on the larger societies of Europe: smaller-scale societies, where some extremely interesting social experiments and theories had been developed, may be more relevant.

Structurally, however, the parallel with Denmark—an agricultural country with strong social democratic traditions—means, according to Arlosoroff that ownership patterns will be much more diffused, decentralized and pluralistic than in the highly industrialized societies; it would also entail strong support, on the financial side, from national sources such as the Zionist Organisation.

The parallel with Denmark also allows Arlosoroff a polemic against the doctrinaire socialist approach which always tended to identify socialism with bureaucratization and centralization, modelled on the large European economies—and, of course, on the Bolshevik example:

> The socialist movement is accused of coercion and domination, based on [narrow] interests. This is highly tendentious. One points to Russia—and overlooks the achievements and innovations of the socialist movement in countries like Denmark and Austria . . .[18]

Arlosoroff concludes by pointing out that the socialist movement in Eretz Israel cannot, consequently, be a sectarian, class-bound movement, but must truly represent the general national effort of the Zionist enterprise. It is the bourgeois Zionist parties who speak for narrow interests, while the linkage between the social and the national in the structure and ideology of the socialist Zionist parties brings about a synthesis between the two elements. If in 1919 Arlosoroff in his essay on Jewish socialism could merely postulate such a synthesis, now, on the evidence of what has actually been done in Palestine, he can revert to this theme, but this time on the basis of concrete historical experience:

> Our party, like the other workers' parties, is made up of different elements: settlers in Degania and Nahalal; workers in the agricultural moshavot—Hadera, Rehovot; railway workers, in constant movement between Qantara and Lydda; clerks and teachers—in Tel Nordau and Beth Hakerem; industrial workers—Nesher [cement] and Nur [matches]; construction workers—Tel Aviv, Afula.
>
> What can unite all these elements? . . . Our party calls for a social ideal which will achieve a national social configuration of the future of our people . . . And I know of no such configuration which is not connected with achieving socialism.[19]

All these disparate elements in the socialist movement in Palestine have not come together in order to achieve a solution for themselves only ('Have we done all this only in order to settle thirty people at Umm Djuni, so that they would live a just life?'). The processes of the formation of a Jewish working class in Palestine were also the processes of the evolution of a Jewish society in the country:

> Within the political reality of Eretz Israel areas of self-government are being established; and this confronts the workers' movement with enterprises of social and political creativity. Is it not clear that when we were confronted in Tel Aviv with the questions of building homes for workers and devising primary education, that our comrades would answer these in the spirit of socialist aspirations? Such a direction of socialist creativity exists also in other areas where no question of class warfare arises.[20]

It is this unity of 'national power and social creativity'

which, according to Arlosoroff, characterized socialist Zionism in the way in which it has actually developed in Eretz Israel, trying to achieve a 'truly liberated society, both in the national and the social sense'.[21] In the concrete context of the historical debate in Palestine between the two main workers' parties (the Marxist Poalei Zion and Hapoel Hatzair), Arlosoroff was truly a unique thinker. While Poalei Zion stressed its internationalist background by being versed in materialism and Marxism, and the more ethically-oriented Hapoel Hatzair shied away from any international context to a degree that sometimes tended to be ethnocentric, Arlosoroff seemed to combine the best of both traditions. He was, on the one hand, imbued with the moral vision of Hapoel Hatzair, yet he felt more at home in the international and cosmopolitan context of the socialist movement than many of the Marxist Zionists, whose internationalism was learned from books and pamphlets and was not grounded in the reality of having lived in a truly international milieu. Arlosoroff was at home both in the Jewish context as well as in the international socialist movement, while being at the same time critical of some of the excesses of the abstract and doctrinaire nature of European socialist thought.

Thus Arlosoroff could locate the particular Jewish quest for a social and national liberation within a wider context of a socialist world of free people—'the new International of free and autonomous nations'.[22] In this he was looking for a redemption for his own people within a universal transformation of society, realizing that in the Jewish case, more so than in others, the national cannot be divorced from the social dimension of human life.

# 7
# CONCLUSION

Arlosoroff did not live to witness either the major catastrophe or the major triumph of Jewish modern life—the Holocaust and the establishment of the State of Israel. We do not know, therefore, how he would have acted under the enormous pressures of these two developments, nor how these events would have shaped his thinking had he been able to experience both the abyss and the apotheosis of Jewish existence during the 1940s.

Yet his writings abound with a deep and tragic premonition that Jewish life as it had existed in Europe for almost two millennia was drawing to a close, and that the Zionist revolution would be successful only if it were able to weave together both the social and the national dimensions of the Jewish renaissance. More than any other Zionist leader or thinker he also felt that Zionism would triumph only if it were able to cultivate a continuous willingness to reach out for a compromise with the Palestinian-Arab national movement—even if this policy were not reciprocated.

The Jewish state as it emerged from the destruction of European Jewry and the onslaught of the surrounding Arab armies was indeed based on these foundations of social reconstruction and a policy of moderation and restraint. The deep current structural problems of Israel can be clearly traced to the country, having gradually adopted different approaches; a retreat from visions of social responsibility was accompanied by an almost unbridled promotion of aggressive individual self-interest, leading to the near-breakdown of many of the country's unique institutions of social co-operation, mutual help and social responsibility. The stock-exchange—that pivot of Jewish financial activity in the Diaspora—has come to substitute the kibbutzim and the pioneers as a symbol of public attention. And, in a parallel fashion, Israel has also witnessed the emergence of vociferous nationalistic policies, devoid of both realism and moderation, which have made reconciliation with the Palestinian Arabs even more difficult. These policies may also turn Israel into a different kind of society, with a tenuous Jewish majority clinging—by sheer force—to its control over a country which may be losing both its Jewish and its democratic character. Politically, these developments have also meant a gradual eclipse of the political movement—the Labour movement—with which Arlosoroff had been identified throughout his life.

A cautionary tale is thus implied in Arlosoroff's thought. The Jewish state he envisioned—humanistic, tolerant, moderate, with a developed social conscience—may be in danger of being replaced by the much more strident mentality of a garrison state. To those who would like, in Israel and abroad, to prevent the Jewish state from embarking on this slippery slope, Arlosoroff's thought should be a source of inspiration and hope for an Israel that, though embattled, still cherishes the universal and Jewish visions which went into its creation as the political expression of the Jewish movement for national liberation.

To an Israel that would still like to be an Athens, and not a Sparta, Arlosoroff—though assassinated—is still alive.

# BIBLIOGRAPHICAL NOTE

There is no full, critical edition of Arlosoroff's writings. It would also be extremely difficult to prepare one, as it would have to be in four languages (German, Hebrew, English and Russian) if every item were to appear in the original language in which it was written.

The seven-volume Hebrew edition, published in 1934 by Mapai to commemorate the first anniversary of Arlosoroff's death, is the most extensive edition of his works. Given the haste in which it was prepared, it was a considerable achievement. It contains most of Arlosoroff's writings, many of his speeches, and numerous letters as well as poems. Those of Arlosoroff's writings which were originally written in Hebrew appear in that language; the rest is translated into Hebrew from the original language in which it was written. But it is far from a complete edition, does not consistently follow critical standards and occasionally the translations leave much to be desired.

The German edition of Arlosoroff's selected works, published in one volume by the Halutz movement in Berlin in 1936 (!) is helpful, but only in a limited fashion. Given the conditions of its publication, the editors had to be careful and cut out extensive passages from various pieces included in the volume, especially those dealing critically with the Revisionist movement, so as not to get into trouble with the Nazi authorities.

We have followed the policy of quoting, in the case of Arlosoroff's main theoretical writings, from the original German editions of his various essays and treatises wherever available. In other cases, we have followed the Hebrew edition, comparing the Hebrew against the original text. In all cases I have prepared my own English translation.

These are the editions used, as well as the abbreviations designating them in the Notes:

| | |
|---|---|
| *Ktavim* | Chaim Arlosoroff, *Ktavim* [Works], ed. Yaacov Steinberg, 7 vols. Tel Aviv, 1934. |
| *JVS* | Viktor Ch. Arlosoroff, *Der jüdische Volkssozialismus*, Berlin, 1919. |
| *KJA* | Dr. Chajim [*sic*] Arlosoroff, *Die Kolonisationsfinanzen der Jewish Agency*, Berlin, 1923. |
| *LW* | Chaim Arlosoroff, *Leben und Werk—Ausgewählte Schriften, Reden, Tagebücher und Briefe*, Berlin, 1936. |
| *YY* | *Yoman Yerushalayim* [Jerusalem Diary], Tel Aviv, 1948. |
| *AHM* | Ascher Maniv, ed. Chaim Arlosoroff, *Am, Hevra u-Medina* [Nation, People and State], with an introduction by Shlomo Avineri, Yad Tabenkin, 1984. |

Among biographies, the most reliable are the Hebrew studies by Yosef Shapiro (1975) and Miriam Getter (1978). The essay by Israel Kolatt in his *Avot u-Meyasdim* [Fathers and Founders], Jerusalem/Tel Aviv, 1975, is also highly recommended. No adequate biography exists in English.

# NOTES

Full bibliographical information will be found in the Bibliographical Note, pp. 115–6.

### 1: *A Brief Life*

1 Chaim Arlosoroff, *Ktavim* [*Works*] Tel Aviv, 1934, VII, p. 134.
2 Chaim Arlosoroff to Professor Goericke (no exact date, 1917), *Ibid.*, VI, pp. 151–2.

### 2: *Class and Nation*

1 Viktor Ch. Arlosoroff, *Der jüdische Volkssozialismus*, Berlin, 1919.
2 *Ktavim*, V, pp. 25–51.
3 *Ibid.*, p. 44.
4 Karl Marx, *Capital*, Moscow, 1959, III, ch. 52, pp. 862–3.
5 *Ktavim*, V, pp. 45ff.
6 *JVS*, pp. 38–9.
7 *Ibid.*, p. 39.
8 *Ibid.*, pp. 40–1.
9 *Ibid.*, p. 11.
10 *Ibid.*
11 *Ibid.*, p. 5.
12 *Ibid.*, pp. 6–7.
13 *Ibid.*, p. 12.
14 *Ibid.*, p. 14.
15 *Ibid.*, pp. 19–21.
16 *Ibid.*, p. 20.
17 *Ibid.*, p. 25.
18 *Ibid.*, p. 23.
19 *Ibid.*, p. 27.
20 *Ibid.*
21 *Ibid.*, pp. 29–30.

22 *Ibid.*, p. 32. Arlosoroff also provides detailed statistical tables about occupational structures in the traditional Jewish Pale of Settlement in Russia–Ukraine and in Galicia.
23 *Ibid.*, pp. 36–7.
24 *Ibid.*, p. 37.
25 *Ibid.*, p. 47.
26 *Ibid.*, p. 48.
27 *Ibid.*, p. 51.
28 *Ibid.*, p. 53. Arlosoroff contrasts these socially-oriented structures of land-owning patterns among the ancient Hebrews with 'the private property of land, which all of Europe inherited from Roman Law and which is the first step in the process whose ultimate result is that the small peasant is driven out from his land into the large urban centre, to sell there his daily labour'. This theme of contrasting Judaic social traditions against European, Gentile private property concepts, is also a favourite theme of Moses Hess. Cf. his 'Über das Geldwesen' ('On Money'), in his *Philosophische und sozialistische Schriften*, ed. W. Mönke, 2nd ed., Vaduz–Berlin/DDR, 1980, pp. 330ff.
29 This is especially pointed out in *JVS*, pp. 55–6.
30 *Ibid.*, p. 56. Arlosoroff devoted a detailed chapter in his memorandum on the finances of the Jewish Agency to this idea. See chapter 3.
31 *Ibid.*, p. 45.
32 *Ibid.*, pp. 58–9.
33 *Ibid.*, p. 59.
34 *Ibid.*, p. 60.
35 *Ibid.*, pp. 61–2.
36 *Ibid.*, p. 63.
37 *Ibid.*, p. 16.

## 3: *Socialism and Nation-Building*

1 Chajim [*sic*] Arlosoroff, *Die Kolonisationsfinanzen der Jewish Agency*, Berlin, 1923.
2 *Ibid.*, pp. 44–5.
3 *Ibid.*, p. 45.
4 *Ibid.*, pp. 14–15. He adds that while socialists usually have plans for expenditure, 'International socialist politics always lacked positive ideas about state income' (p. 16).
5 *Ibid.*, p. 21.
6 *Ibid.*, pp. 24–5.
7 *Ibid.*, p. 26.

8 *Ibid.*, p. 36.
9 *Ibid.*, p. 51.
10 Arlosoroff mentions, among others, Richard Lichtheim (pp. 50–1).
11 *Ibid.*, pp. 52–3.
12 *Ibid.*, p. 94.
13 *Ibid.*, pp. 98–9. In this analysis of colonial settlement, Arlosoroff frequently refers to his teacher Werner Sombart, and especially to his *Modern Capitalism*.
14 *KJA*, p. 61.
15 *Ibid.*, p. 83. In an interesting comment Arlosoroff compares his proposal to the voluntary taxation of the Greek Diaspora during the Greek struggle of independence, but finds a fundamental difference: the Greeks did, after all, possess an existing Greek society, whereas in the Jewish case, such a society had still to be created (p. 84).
16 *Ibid.*, pp. 155–67. The idea of a note-issuing Jewish bank is of course the most far-reaching proposal in the memorandum, and Arlosoroff feels he has to justify his belief that it is both financially feasible and will be permitted by the British administration. It should be remembered that at that time private banks in several European countries still issued paper money against gold and silver deposits, and Arlosoroff gives the example, in pre-1914 Germany, of the banks of Bavaria, Saxony and Württemberg, which were allowed to issue paper money. He also refers to examples in pre-1776 British North America.
17 *Ibid.*, p. 196.
18 'Zur Struktur der Vierten Alijah,' in: Chaim Arlosoroff, *Leben und Werk*, Berlin, 1936, p. 125.
19 *Ibid.*, p. 126.
20 *Ibid.*, p. 127.
21 *Ibid.*, p. 128.
22 'The Economic Conditions of the Yishuv,' *Ktavim*, II, p. 29.
23 'Zur Struktur, etc.', *LW*, p. 129.
24 *Ibid.*, p. 130.
25 *Ibid.*, p. 133. Arlosoroff mistakenly writes 'East End' in referring to New York's East Side.
26 *Ibid.*, p. 132.
27 *Ibid.*, p. 133.
28 *Ibid.*, pp. 133–4.
29 *Ibid.*, p. 134.
30 See *Ktavim*, II, pp. 23–42.
31 See 'Konsequenzen,' in *LW*, pp. 136–52.

32 *Ibid.*, p. 140ff.
33 *Ibid.*, p. 142.
34 *Ibid.*, pp. 142–3. One of Arlosoroff's suggestions to overcome this is by raising the minimum capital necessary for a 'capitalist' certificate of immigration from £500 to £800, so as to minimize the danger of further business failures due to under-capitalization. While other Zionist leaders, many of them members of the bourgeois General Zionists, called, sometimes demogogically, for the abolition of any limits on immigration, the socialist Arlosoroff, with his knowledge of political economy, advocated a more careful approach, realizing that a higher minimum might be required. For him, more sometimes meant less. For the demagogues, such mundane considerations did not matter.
35 *Ibid.*, p. 146.
36 *Ibid.*, p. 145.
37 *Ibid.*, p. 146.
38 *Ibid.*, p. 148.
39 *Ibid.*, p. 149.
40 *Ibid.*, p. 151.

## 4: *Between Jew and Arab*

1 See the recent study of Yosef Gorny, *Zionism and the Arabs—A Study of Ideology*, Oxford, 1987. Also Shmuel Almog (ed.), *Zionism and the Arabs*, Jerusalem, 1983.
2 *JVS*, p. 50.
3 'The Events of May', *Ktavim*, I, p. 6.
4 *Ibid.*, p. 8.
5 *Ibid.*, p. 7.
6 *Ibid.*, p. 9.
7 *Ibid.*, p. 8.
8 *Ibid.*
9 *Ibid.*, p. 9.
10 *Ibid.*, pp. 9–10.
11 *Ibid.*, p. 10.
12 *KJA*, p. 35.
13 Chaim Arlosoroff to his wife Sima, 24 August, 1929, in *LW*, pp. 273–4. How much Arlosoroff had been distancing himself from any political involvement with the controversy surrounding the Wailing Wall can also be seen from a much more guarded passage in a speech made at the Albert Hall in London, a few days later in commemoration of the Jews murdered in the riots:

'This assembly has, in my view, to tell the whole world that we wish to build, in a few years, not one, ancient and age-eaten Wall in order to pray and wail at it, but thousands of walls of new homes for our *halutzim* who will live in them and, if necessary, defend them' (*Ktavim*, VI, p. 70). The whole 'constructivist' philosophy of Arlosoroff is encapsulated in this juxtaposition of activist construction against harping on symbols of the historical past.

14 The following is a condensed summing up of Arlosoroff's opening argument in 'Versuch eines Resumés,' *LW*, pp. 153–4.

15 *Ibid.*, p. 156.

16 *Ktavim*, I, p. 105. This passage is not included in the German edition of *Leben und Werke*, obviously out of consideration for the fact that the volume was published in Germany in 1936 under Nazi rule.

17 *LW*, pp. 158–9. The comment on the Islamic-Communist alliance transcends the immediate conditions of 1929: 'One should not be surprised by the Communists, who have declared this outpouring of hatred instigated by the Mufti and the clerical Muslim reactionaries to be a "national revolution". In the Orient, the Communists have consistently been the allies of the extreme chauvinistic groups.' (*Ibid.*, p. 158).

18 *Ibid.*, pp. 162–3.

19 *Ibid.*, p. 164. After Arlosoroff's death, Ben Gurion tried to follow a similar line of an opening to Arab leaders inside and outside Palestine; see Shabtai Teveth, *Ben Gurion and the Palestinian Arabs*, New York, 1985.

20 *LW*, p. 165. The first Jewish students from Palestine were indeed sent shortly afterwards by the Jewish Agency to study, at the American University in Beirut, the centre of Arab secular nationalism (then as much as now).

21 *Ktavim*, I, p. 120. These paragraphs, as well as other critical remarks by Arlosoroff on the Revisionists, are not included in the 1936 German edition of *Leben und Werke*, published in Berlin under Nazi rule (on p. 164 the editors remark that 'the Jewish factor will not be discussed in the framework of this edition'.) Obviously the similarity of Arlosoroff's critique of the style and substance of Revisionism was too close to some obvious criticism of Nazism; the editors, who had to navigate carefully when publishing this volume under Nazi rule, preferred not to stretch the limits of what would be allowed to them under Nazi censorship.

22 *LW*, p. 163.

23 A background study by Arlosoroff which triggered these initiatives can be found in his 'The Economic Foundations of the Arab Problem' (1930), *LW*, pp. 172–83.
24 For the text of the speeches, see Chaim Arlosoroff, *Am, Hevra u-Medina*, ed. Asher Maniv, Yad Tabenkin, 1984, pp. 172–4. The original text of the Zionist Executive speech is in the Central Zionist Archives in Jerusalem and that of the Mapai speech in the Mapai Archives at Beit Berl.

## 5: *Confronting the British Empire*

1 *Ktavim*, I, p. 71.
2 *Ibid.*, p. 73.
3 *Ibid.*, p. 74.
4 *Ibid.*, pp. 76–7.
5 *Ibid.*, pp. 78–9.
6 The full text was published for the first time in 1984 *AHM*.
7 *Ibid.*, p. 119.
8 *Ibid.*, p. 120.
9 *Ibid.*, pp. 122–3.
10 *Ibid.*, pp. 125–126.
11 *Ibid.*, p. 129.
12 *Ktavim*, V, pp. 7–51. See also chapter 6.
13 *Ktavim*, IV, esp. pp. 254–64, where he discusses the modernization imposed on India by the British East India Company.
14 *AHM*, pp. 131–2. In a pointed analogy, nicely targeted at his Labour Party audience, Arlosoroff compares those who oppose utilizing the emerging state machinery in Palestine to the machine-smashing Luddites at the outset of the Industrial Revolution.
15 *Ibid.*, p. 133.
16 The full original English text of the letter has never been published, and it is being quoted here from the carbon copy in the Central Zionist Archives (File S25/795). The original is in the Weizmann Archives in Rehovot. A Hebrew translation has been included in *YY* and reprinted in *AHM*, pp. 160–70.
17 See, e.g. Israel Kolatt's fine attempt at a synthesis in the chapter on Arlosoroff, 'The Making of a Statesman', in his *Avot u-Meyasdim* [Fathers and Founders], Jerusalem/Tel–Aviv, 1975, pp. 63–84.
18 We have already seen earlier, in chapter 4, how these considerations would lead Arlosoroff in late 1932 and early 1933 to try to purchase land in Transjordan.

## 6: *Future Society: A Federation of Free Communist Associations*

1 *Ktavim*, VI, p. 32.
2 *Ibid.*, pp. 10–11.
3 *Ibid.* The socialist movement did, however, according to Arlosoroff's acute observation, pay a price for its success as a mass movement: 'only when the sect gradually becomes a party and the movement turns into a strong organization, does the anonymous member replace the individual: the masses of voters, the multitude of members. The inner nature of leadership also changes fundamentally, leading up to the emergence of a party bureaucracy.' In this and other instances it is evident that Arlosoroff has been following some of the ideas of Roberto Michels on the bureaucratization of European social-democratic parties.
4 *Ibid.*, p. 20.
5 *Ibid.*, p. 19.
6 *Ibid.*, pp. 21–2. On this occassion Arlosoroff also refers to Kropotkin seeing in the Russian village communes (the *mir*) a nucleus of socialist development.
7 *Ibid.*, p. 22.
8 *Ibid.*, p. 24.
9 *Ibid.*, p. 25.
10 *Ibid.*, p. 32.
11 *Ibid.*, pp. 27–30.
12 *Ibid.*, p. 30.
13 *Ibid.*, pp. 32–3.
14 See above in chapter 2.
15 *Ktavim*, III, pp. 123–4. With characteristic candour and sociological insight, Arlosoroff adds: 'If there exists a proletariat [in Palestine] which sees itself without public standing and appreciation, it is to be found among the Oriental communities and in Mea Shearim [the ultra orthodox neighbourhood].' Many decades later, the Labour Party in Israel would pay a heavy political price for overlooking this aspect of Israeli social reality, which became even more intensive after 1948, with the influx of new immigrants form Middle Eastern countries. Before 1948, it was these groups which were also the social basis of recruitment for the right-wing underground organizations, IZL (the 'Irgun') and LHY (the so–called Stern Group).
16 *Ibid.*, p. 126.
17 *Ibid.*, p. 127–8.
18 *Ibid.*, p. 129.

19 *Ibid.*, p. 131.
20 *Ibid.*
21 *Ibid.*, p. 132.
22 *JVS*, p. 15.

# INDEX